TALKING GERMANY

TALKING GERMANY

Jennifer Lee

rosters

Published by ROSTERS LTD.

23 Welbeck Street, London W1M 7PG

© Jennifer Lee

ISBN 0-948032-78-2

First Edition 1990

Designed and published by ROSTERS
Typeset by JH Graphics Ltd, Reading, Berks
Printed and bound in Great Britain by Cox & Wyman Ltd, Reading

Acknowledgements

My thanks are due to my publisher, Rosemary Burr, for her interest, help and encouragement and to Sally Parkin and Sally Lee for their assistance in checking and proof reading. Most of all, to my husband, John Lee, for all his help, his patient editing and for contributing Chapters Five and Eight.

Every possible care has been taken to ensure the accuracy of the information in this book. I am particularly grateful to Jeanette Schuchmann and her staff at the German National Tourist Office who cheerfully answered my queries and allowed me to use information from their many helpful brochures. However, in the travel industry at the moment, nothing is static and neither the German National Tourist Office nor the author or publishers can accept responsibility for any changes, errors or omissions which may have occurred.

Dedication

To my chauffeur, cartographer, adviser, companion, contributor, editor and long suffering husband. To John with love and gratitude.

Foreword

You will find no authoritative (and boring) descriptions of cathedrals and architectural wonders in this new guide to Germany. No lists of five star hotels which few holiday-makers can afford! But lots of advice, gathered over many holiday trips, some hints for those venturing into Germany for the first time and some slightly reluctant revelations of places we have discovered and enjoyed.

If you are tired of package holidays and waiting around in airports, if you have enjoyed motoring holidays in France, why not try something different — why not Germany?

Contents

Part One:
Getting to know Germany

Part Two:
Motoring Tours

Part Three:
Holidays without a car

Part One:
Getting to know Germany

CHAPTER ONE:
WHY NOT GERMANY?

Summer on an East Frisian Island

It is the height of summer at the seaside but there is not a car to be seen or heard! Just miles of sandy beach, the flap of the sails of the land yachts, the cries of sea birds and the tinkle of bicycle bells along the paths through the sand dunes. Why no cars? Simply because they have to be left on the mainland as motor vehicles are not permitted on most of these peaceful islands which lie off the coast between the *Ems* and the *Weser* estuaries.

Winter in Cologne

Another time of year and another place. It is winter and the streets of *Cologne* are packed with revellers catching showers of sweets and other goodies thrown from hundreds of decorated floats escorted by brass bands and bevies of exuberant clowns. It is *Karneval* on Rose Monday — the day before Shrove Tuesday at the beginning of Lent — but you will not notice the cold as you join in the dancing in the streets and sip the warming *Glühwein*. The Germans really love Karneval and at least a quarter of the watching crowd — adults and tiny tots alike — are dressed in clown costumes with faces painted to match. A marvellous day out for the whole family.

Any time

Summer or winter, country or city — Germany can provide a setting for almost any kind of holiday and yet it is still relatively unexplored by British holiday makers. In several years touring in Germany we have been amazed at how few GB plates we see. Cross-channel motorists generally head straight off to Spain or the Côte d'Azur or tour the well-known areas of France unaware that Germany has just as much to offer tourists. The only difficulty is to decide where to go first!

● Mountains

You could enjoy the view from the top of a mountain and decide whether to walk back down through the trees and over the grassy slopes or ride back down in the cable car over the tops of the forest, getting a better view of that turreted castle glimpsed through the trees.

● Skiing

If you are a skiing enthusiast you can find facilities just as plentiful as in Switzerland, but far less expensive. Cross-country trails, ski jumps, lifts to high Alpine snowfields or smooth nursery slopes are all available in *Black Forest* resorts, *East Bavarian* villages or Alpine centres near the Austrian border.

● Lovely lakes

You might prefer to stroll along the promenade on the shore of an emerald blue lake dotted with the multi-coloured sails of yachts and wind surfers and crossed by white-painted ferry boats – or swim in the warm, clear waters. Choose *Lake Constance*, the mountain lakes of *Upper Bavaria* or the Lake District of *Schleswig Holstein*.

● Wine tasting and river cruises

For a relaxing holiday, try a wine-tasting tour through famous vineyards or sip a glass of the local wine as you recline on the deck of a ship cruising, not through empty seas, but down a wide river whose banks are lined with vines, fairy-tale castles and attractive villages where you can stop for a stroll.

● Fitness and nature trails

If you want more strenuous activity, test yourself on a fitness trail while the rest of the family enjoy a less demanding nature walk in a peaceful forest close to the border with eastern Europe. Or wander along the well planned and sign-posted footpaths of the *Black Forest*.

● Festivals

Join in the fun at a village festival or pageant. You can find one at almost any time of the year. Religious and historical celebrations, beer or wine festivals − every town and village will have a list of events throughout the year. These are mainly for their own enjoyment but they will be happy to welcome you as well.

● Shopping and sight-seeing

Go shopping in some of the most exclusive and well-stocked cities in Europe; sightseeing in towns famous in history and legend; visit Roman remains in *Trier* or *Xanten*; or the walled medieval towns of the *Romantic Road*, little changed since the fourteenth century.

● Spoil yourself at a spa

Stay in one of the many attractive spa towns where you can take the waters or an "anti-stress" cure, be cosseted and massaged, lose weight, take exercise by practising your favourite sporting activity or simply relax in luxurious sur-roundings amid beautiful scenery with a healthy climate and listen to the spa orchestra playing in the park.

A wide choice

These are just a few of the holidays of many different kinds waiting to be explored and enjoyed. There is an enormous choice and it is a difficult decision.

It all depends what you want from a holiday. Do you enjoy driving? Do you want to see as many places as possible? If you do, you could link together parts of several of the tours suggested in this book and see many different areas of the

country. Do you prefer to find somewhere to settle? Then choose your destination and plan an interesting route.

Help from the German National Tourist Office
Decide what you really want from your holiday — and what you do not! Get all the information you can, rule out the places which do not appeal to you and then decide on the area which takes your fancy. Write to the **German National Tourist Office at** *65 Curzon Street, London W1Y 7PE (Tel. 01-495-3990)*. If you do not want to go it alone and prefer a package holiday ask specifically for their leaflet **Inclusive Holiday Digest**. You are almost certain to find a company offering a holiday you would enjoy.

Planning your own holiday
If you prefer to "do-it-yourself", ask for general brochures and additional information on any areas you are particularly interested in. The attractive leaflets you will receive will help you to come to more detailed decisions.

Help from tourist offices in Germany
Then you will need more local information. In Appendix 1 you will find addresses of the regional tourist offices of the main holiday areas. You will notice from the addresses given that a Tourist Information Office can be known by various names:

It may be called a *Verkehrsverband*, a *Fremdenverkehrsverband (FVV)*, a *Landesverkehrsverband*, a *Verkehrsamt*, a *Verkehrsbüro*, or a *Verkehrsverein*. They all seem to be uniformly helpful and prompt in their replies. Their information will help you to decide on possible areas to visit and routes to get there.

Accommodation lists
If you are travelling independently by car, you will also need regional accommodation lists for finding overnight accommodation on your journey. It is always difficult to tell just how far you are likely to travel on any particular day.

You may find interesting places to explore, you may find an idyllic picnic place for a long lunch-break, there may be diversions or delays or the area may not be as attractive as you expected. If you are equipped with these regional lists your choice is left open until you decide on the right time and place to stop.

Local information offices

If you are particularly attracted to certain towns or villages, write to the FVV of that town and you will be sent detailed information. In tourist areas, each town or village, however small, seems to publish a colour brochure and list of serviced and self-catering accommodation giving details of prices, number of rooms which have private bathrooms etc. Most small towns and villages also have a compact and well-kept campsite.

How to write for information

Write to those which you feel might be of interest to you. I'm sure they will reply if you write in English but if you prefer to write in German here is the letter we use. It may not be grammatically correct but it gets the required results!

> *Sehr geehrte Herren*
> *Dieses Jahr fahren wir für unser Urlaub nach Deutschland und höffentlich werden wir Ihr Gegend besuchen.*
>
> *Könnten Sie mir bitte Informationen schicken, zum Beispiel:*
>
> *Hotel u. Pensionverzeichnis*
> *Broschüren*
> *Veranstaltungskalenderen für (August)*
> *Karten/Stadtpläne u.s.w.*
>
> *Ich danke Ihnen für Ihr Entgegenkommen.*
>
> *Mit freundlichen Grüssen*

In it we ask for tourist information including a list of hotels and guest houses, brochures, calendar of events for the month we shall be visiting, and town plans and maps.

Choosing maps

Once you have decided on a particular area or route you will need a detailed map. Really good maps are not easy to find. There is nothing to compare with our Ordnance Survey series but the Michelin Red Map 987 covering Germany, Austria and the Benelux countries will give you an overall view to plan your route and Michelin 984 shows Germany on a slightly larger scale. There is a new Michelin series now available (1990) covering Germany in three sections: 411 Northern Germany, 412 Central Germany and 413 Bavaria and Baden Württemberg (1cm:4km). For some areas bordering France and Switzerland you will be able to find a yellow larger scale Michelin (1cm:2km). A good map shop may also supply *JRO Verlagsgesellshaft* maps for various areas of Germany or *Deutsche Reisekarte* (published by *Kümmerly + Frey*). You do need maps — otherwise you will be stuck to motorways and main roads and you will miss most of the best places.

High standards

Whichever kind of holiday you choose, you will find everywhere clean, tidy and well cared for. There are good amenities — and facilities (including conveniences!) are of a high standard. The people are friendly and helpful and accommodation of all kinds is available at reasonable prices. So why not Germany next time?

CHAPTER TWO:
GETTING THERE

Germany is relatively easy to get to. In fact, from Dover, the Rhine Valley is much nearer than the Lake District. Germany is about half as big as France or Spain — about 550 miles from north to south and just over 250 miles from east to west.

The Federal not the Democratic Republic

Throughout this book "Germany" means "West Germany", or to give its official name, the German *Federal* Republic. It is now increasingly possible to visit East Germany — the German *Democratic* Republic — but at the time of writing, it still entails complications such as obtaining a visa and supplying detailed addresses of the places where you intend to stay each night though these restrictions are expected to be eased. Visits to West Berlin will probably also become easier as the journey through East Germany may become less regulated. It should even be possible to visit East Berlin now that the wall has been opened up.

Independent or packaged?

Germany is not yet high on the list of destinations advertised by travel agents. Nevertheless, "packages" of all kinds, catering for many different types of traveller with varied interests, are available from a range of smaller companies.

There are plenty of coach tours to the most scenic areas, city visits or short breaks by air, resort holidays (by air, rail or with your own car), self-catering holidays, hotel tours,

18

cruises, cycle or motor cycle tours, walking, caravan or camping holidays. There are also some companies who arrange visits to special events, including important sporting dates. You can book a wine or beer tour or a specially planned holiday for the disabled; a visit to the *Cologne Carnival* or the *Munich Beer Festival*; a language course or tours of the battlefields; special interest holidays for railway or travel enthusiasts. The German National Tourist Office can supply a list of over 200 travel companies offering holidays of every kind.

If you prefer to be independent and "do your own thing" there is no difficulty. Once you have decided where you want to go, pick a ferry or an airport, plan your route by car, coach or rail and ask the German National Tourist Office for lists of suitable accommodation. No package can ever be as individually planned as the one you arrange for yourself. You can go where you choose, when you choose and do what you choose!

Ferry routes

Scandinavian Seaways (DFDS): There are many ferry routes to the Continent but only one which goes directly to Germany. Scandinavian Seaways, which until recently was called DFDS, operates between Harwich and *Hamburg*. The crossing takes 21 hours but if you live in East Anglia or the North and plan to visit Northern Germany this could be the most convenient, and possibly more economical if you take into account savings on petrol and en route accommodation.

North Sea Ferries: For Northerners, there are also overnight crossings from Hull to Rotterdam or Zeebrugge by North Sea Ferries. The Rotterdam crossing will take you well on your way if you are planning to visit Northern Germany, while Zeebrugge is more convenient for travelling further south.

Sealink: Those living north of Watford might also find the Sealink crossing from Harwich to the Hook of Holland useful, particularly when travelling to northern or central Germany. If you live in the South or are off to the central or southern parts of Germany, consider the other Sealink crossings from Dover to Calais or Folkestone to Boulogne though you will probably feel that the Dutch and Belgian ports have rather better motorway links.

P & O: Crossings from Felixstowe to Zeebrugge; Dover to Ostend, Zeebrugge, Calais or Boulogne. On the longer Portsmouth to Le Havre route you can travel by day or overnight.

Sally Line: Economical crossings from Ramsgate to Dunkerque. If you have a family party in a car one child under 14 is carried free on any sailing. There is also a Car + 5 passengers special return fare.

Hoverspeed: They will take you across from Dover to Boulogne or Calais in thirty-five minutes. They also have a special family rate for two adults and two children.

Olau Line: Our favourite is the Olau Line crossing to Holland from Sheerness to Vlissingen. The Olau Line boats are more cruise liner than ferry and, though the crossing is longer than the Dover/Calais route, the accommodation is spacious and comfortable. If you choose to cross at night a cabin gives a restful start to your holiday.

Rail travel

You can book an International Rail route from London Victoria via Dover and Ostend or from Liverpool Street to the Hook of Holland connecting with excellent train services to all parts of Germany.

There is a motorail network which is fully integrated with the rest of the European motorail services. Long-distance overnight trains have sleeping car services complete with showers and air-conditioning. Beds are bookable in advance though some trains provide couchettes instead.

By coach

National Express, in association with Eurolines and Transline, runs international coaches from London ·and Cardiff to various destinations in Germany. Euroline has a service through *Aachen, Cologne, Frankfurt, Mannheim, Stuttgart* and *Nuremberg* to *Munich* which takes about twenty-four hours. There is another route via Amsterdam to *Leer, Oldenburg, Bremen, Hamburg* and *Travemünde*, which takes about the same time. Transline runs a service from Cardiff and London to many places in Northern Germany including *Brunswick, Celle, Dortmund, Düsseldorf, Essen, Hamelin* and *Hanover*.

Full details of all these services are available from National Coach booking offices or by writing to **Eurolines (UK) Ltd,** 23 Crawley Road, Luton, LU1 1HX Tel: 0582 404511. There is also an International Express Helpline on 0582 62545.

By air

Flights are available with several different airlines from London to *Hamburg, Bremen, Hanover, Düsseldorf, Münster, Stuttgart, Cologne/Bonn, Frankfurt, Nuremberg* and *Munich*. There are also BA and *Lufthansa* flights to *Hamburg* from Aberdeen, Birmingham, Glasgow, and Manchester: to *Cologne/Bonn* from Birmingham, Belfast and Edinburgh: to *Münster* from Glasgow and Manchester and to *Munich* and *Hanover* from Belfast, Birmingham, Glasgow and Manchester.

Other airlines have services from Birmingham, Bristol, Manchester, Glasgow and Edinburgh to *Düsseldorf* and *Frankfurt* while *Nuernberger Flugdienst* fly from Manchester to *Nuremberg*. British Air Ferries and Birmingham Executive Airways will take you to *Stuttgart* from Birmingham airport. All these destinations can be reached in less than one hour 40 minutes. The airports have excellent communications with the cities by public transport and, of course, car hire is always available, bookable in advance in the UK if you prefer.

21

Plan your route

It is probably better to put off making a definite decision on your journey until you have made up your mind which part of Germany you plan to visit and how you intend to get there. Only you know how far — and how fast — you wish to travel, how much time you have available both before and after your crossing, and — if you plan to take your car — how experienced you are at Continental driving. Try not to travel too far in one day. Remember that half the fun is seeing the countryside along the way.

CHAPTER THREE:
DECIDING WHERE TO STAY

If you are travelling independently you will discover that finding accommodation in Germany is seldom a problem. We never book ahead but even at the height of the holiday season in July and August we have not had any real difficulty, although I must admit we seldom try to stay in the larger towns or resorts.

Prices

Germany has not suffered high inflation over the past few years and prices seem to have remained virtually the same since our first visits nearly ten years ago. It is still possible to find a room in a *Gasthaus* near beautiful *Lake Constance* for under £7 a night per person and even a room with a private bathroom for less than £10, although in big cities like *Hamburg* or *Cologne* you would have to search hard to find accommodation at that price. For little more than £100 for a week in summer you could find a chalet for four people in a *Bavarian Forest* holiday park complete with indoor pool, sauna/solarium and lots of other facilities.

Accommodation lists

If you plan to arrange your own accommodation, the German National Tourist Office in London will send you a thick brochure called **"Holidays in Germany; Accommodation Catalogue for Hotels, Inns and Boarding Houses"**. This gives a small selection of the accommodation available in each region and will enable you to see what kinds of facilities and prices you are likely to find. The prices quoted are mainly for stays of seven or three days.

Among the brochures you will receive if you write to a local tourist office or *Verkehrsamt* will be lists of all kinds of establishments which offer accommodation to the visitor or tourist, with details of facilities and price ranges for overnight stays.

Small hotels

As well as hotels you may see listed a *Hotel Garni*. These provide rooms and breakfast but no other meals. A *Pension* is a boarding or guest house while a *Gasthaus* or *Gasthof* is an inexpensive type of inn whose main business is meals but which has a limited number of rooms.

Castle hotels

If you are feeling a little more affluent you may be interested in the "Castle Hotels". These are old castles, some privately owned, which have been turned into hotels. They are not all particularly sumptuous, but some are very luxurious. Whatever the standard, the atmosphere and furnishings are reputed to be authentic. A list of these *Schlosshotels* can be obtained from the German Tourist Office or by writing to: **Gast im Schloss e.V., D-3526 Trendelburg 1. West Germany.**

If you prefer a package, **Unicorn Holidays** have a programme of holidays staying in these hotels travelling with your own car or flying to a convenient airport and using a hire car.

Romantik Hotels

Another interesting group is known as the *Romantik Hotels*. There are over 50 of these, generally in country areas, and are all said to be "brimming with charm and comfort". They are in historic buildings and claim to offer first-class cuisine with friendly service and a homely atmosphere. The prices range from fairly cheap to very expensive. A full list can be obtained from: *Romantik Hotels KG, Freigerichtstrasse 5, D-8757 Karlstein-a-M., West Germany.*

Other hotel chains
The ferry companies, the RAC and some other travel firms have arrangements with some of the European hotel chains and will book an inclusive holiday for you if you wish.

Several of the hotel chains in this country have links with hotels in Germany and will gladly book accommodation for you. A list of addresses will be found in Appendix 2.

Or you could contact the **German Hotel Reservation Service — ADZ —** a non-profit making organisation of the German National Tourist Board who will arrange reservations of all categories in cities and holiday resorts for visitors to Germany. Their address is: *DZT-Service Department ADZ; German Hotel Reservation Service, Corneliusstrasse 34, D-6000 Frankfurt/Main 1, West Germany.*

Bed and breakfast
If you are travelling without pre-booked accommodation, keep an eye open for *Zimmer frei* or *Fremdenheim* signs. These indicate a room to let in a private house — what we would call "bed and breakfast". Those we have tried have been very comfortable and well equipped, in some most attractive locations and very inexpensive.

Ask to see the room
All of these establishments will gladly show you which rooms they have available. You just ask *"Haben Sie ein Zimmer frei bitte?"* (Have you a room available please?) and unless they are full, they will gladly take you to look around.

Checking the price
It is a requirement that the price of each room shall be displayed inside the room itself so on your "look around" take the opportunity to check the price. And remember that the price mentioned is for the room — not per person. Breakfast,

25

Frühstück, is sometimes charged separately though service charges and taxes are usually included.

Motorway motels

On the motorways you will find *Rasthausen* — like our Service Areas but generally much cleaner and of a higher standard. Some of these have motel rooms. A folder obtainable from the German National Tourist Office and called "Autobahn Service" shows the entire motorway system and all facilities available.

Standards are high

Even if a hotel is not mentioned in your tourist office list it does not necessarily mean there is anything wrong with it. The general standard of accommodation is uniformly high. Even the cheapest rooms will be spotlessly clean and well equipped with bedding and fittings of a high quality and most will have private bathroom facilities, or at least a shower cubicle — though not always soap, so take your own just in case.

Blind to the blinds!

The furnishings are always so good we were amazed one evening when settling down in our tiny country inn room — beautiful bedclothes, well fitted shower etc. — to find that the very attractive curtains would not close when pulled. As the window was overlooked by houses on the other side of the road we pinned the curtains together with a safety pin in the interests of modesty, very surprised at this lapse in comfort. In the morning we were embarrassed to realise that the window was fitted with outside shutters operated by a pulley at the side of the window. We had seen these everywhere but had not been bright enough to look for them the night before. Just a point to bear in mind!

Help from the Tourist Office

Should you arrive in a busy resort late in the evening and have difficulty in finding accommodation, ask at the Tourist

Office and they will telephone round for you and almost certainly find you somewhere pleasant. On one occasion on the shores of *Lake Constance* the young lady working in the office took us home to her mother's farmhouse when almost everything was full.

Farm holidays

If you prefer to stay in one place you might enjoy a farm holiday – *Ferien auf dem Bauernhof*. Ask for a list at the German National Tourist Office or at the local tourist office. These leaflets are only available in German and they suggest that anyone booking this type of holiday should have at least a basic knowledge of the language.

If you have no German but would like a farm holiday, **Scandinavian Seaways** have some farmhouse holidays which you can book either as self-catering or half-board accommodation.

Self-catering accommodation

If you are interested in self-catering accommodation – *Ferienwohnungen* or *Ferienhäuser* – ask the German National Tourist Office for the brochure **"Self-catering in Germany; Chalets, villas, apartments and holiday-villages"**. There is a wide range available from chalets or apartments in organised holiday villages to apartments in hotel blocks or individual villas or houses - usually in very beautiful places.

Self-catering packages are also available from the ferry companies, the **German Travel Agency** and other travel firms such as **Auto Plan, Hoseasons, Cosmos, Heartland Holidays, Interhome Limited, Overdrive, Tourauto** and **David Newman's European Collection.**

Youth hostels

There are 600 Youth Hostels, many in fantastic settings such as the one in the *Stahleck* fortress above the village of *Bacharach* in the most beautiful part of the Rhine Valley. They are open to members of any youth hostel association

affiliated to the International Youth Hostels Association. A full list and further details are available from:
Deutsches Jugendherbergswerk, Bülowstrasse 26, Postfach 220, 4930 Detmold, West Germany.

Camping and caravanning

There are over 2000 camping sites in Germany, generally open from April to October, though in winter sport areas there are about 400 sites which stay open all year. A free map and folder giving details of hundreds of selected camp sites throughout the country is available from the German National Tourist Office.

It is not often possible to book in advance if you are travelling independently but **Select Site Reservations** will arrange bookings on sites throughout the country from *Cuxhaven* on the North Sea coast to *Viechtach* and *Zwiesel* in *East Bavaria,* and *Staufen* in the *Black Forest*.

Eurocamp Travel Ltd and **Canvas Holidays** also have a site reservation service for independent travellers. For those without their own equipment, they also have ready-erected tents on selected sites in several attractive parts of the country.

If you wish to camp anywhere outside of an official campsite, the permission of the farmer and /or the local police must be obtained. The address of the **German Camping Club** is: **Deutscher Camping-Club, Mandelstrasse 28, 8000 München 40, West Germany.**

The Caravan Club have holidays for their members using their own cars and vans in the *Lahn Valley* and *Black Forest*. They also have a combined caravanning and cruising holiday in the *Rhine* and *Mosel* valleys.

Canterbury Travel have fly/drive holidays where you fly to *Frankfurt* and collect a camper.

Scandinavian Seaways also have mobile homes which you can hire after crossing on one of their ferries.

Package holidays

These are among the most economical ways to have a holiday in Germany. Many of the coach holiday companies offer attractive trips to the *Rhine Valley*, the *Romantic Road* or the *Black Forest*. You will find a list in Chapter Nineteen.

If you prefer to travel by car the ferry companies have a wide choice of holidays as do some of the smaller travel companies listed in the **Holiday Digest** from the German National Tourist Office. If you are nervous about setting out without a prospective roof to go over the heads of your family why not try one of these for your first foray into Germany?

CHAPTER FOUR:
WHAT TO TAKE WITH YOU

Currency

You will need some German money. The basic currency in Germany is the *Deutschmark (DM)* which is divided into 100 *Pfennigs*. There are notes worth 5, 10, 20, 50, 100, 500 and 1000 *DM*. Coins are for 1, 2 and 5 *DM* and 1, 2, 5, 10 and 50 *Pfennigs,* although the smaller coins are of little practical use nowadays except for parking meters and toilets.

You can buy *DM* either here at a bank or travel agent or, increasingly possible now, at a building society — or you can leave it until you are on the boat or have arrived in Germany. Whichever you choose to do, it pays to look at the boards displaying the current exchange rates in one or two different places. Remember you will be "buying" *DM* — so look under the column headed "we sell". They also charge a commission on every transaction so look for or ask how much that is. One or two building societies make no charge or just a nominal charge to their members. Most banks charge a flat rate of between £1 and £1.50 per £100 changed and/or a commission of 1% or 1½%.

If you are travelling at a weekend (a practice to be avoided if at all possible as ferries are crowded and more expensive, and the roads on both sides of the Channel very busy!) remember that German banks, like British ones, will be closed. However you will probably find an Exchange Bureau open at the border or at the largest railway stations or airports if you are really stuck.

Travellers cheques, Eurocheques and Postcheques

If you do not wish to take all your money in *DM* you will have to decide whether to take Travellers cheques, Eurocheques or Postcheques to supplement the cash you take with you for immediate needs.

Travellers cheques are obtainable from banks, some travel agents and from building societies. Wherever you get them, unless you are lucky enough to find a special offer, you will have to pay a commission usually of 1% or 1½%. Once again it is the smaller building societies which may offer Travellers cheques free of charge or at a low commission. Travellers cheques provide some insurance against loss as the issuing company, usually American Express or Thomas Cook, will replace them — while you are still on holiday in most cases. You can take *Deutschmark* travellers cheques, which may mean a better rate of exchange and smaller charges when you cash them in Germany — though not if you bring them back home again.

Eurocheques are bought from your bank. To obtain a Eurocard, which acts as a cheque guarantee card, you will be asked to pay an annual fee of between £4 and £6 depending on which bank you use. There will then be a commission of about 1.6% plus a handling fee of about 30p charged when your bank account is debited back in this country. The banks say that if you are charged a commission or fee when you cash your Eurocheque abroad they will refund the amount charged if you provide a receipt. With Eurocheques you can draw cheques in *DM* to pay hotel bills or for purchases instead of having to change them in banks but you will not know exactly how much you have paid until the conversion into sterling has been done at your own bank.

Postcheques are supplied only by Girobank. They are similar to standard cheques and have to be backed up with a Postcheque card which is supplied free with your first batch of cheques. They can be used to withdraw cash in local currency at post offices in Germany.

Credit cards

Most banks in Germany will accept your credit card and advance you cash with no handling charge, but remember that you will be charged interest straightaway.

You will find that large hotels and stores in major cities will accept most credit cards but otherwise cards are not so readily and universally acceptable in German shops, hotels and petrol stations as they are in Britain. Some stores will indicate that they accept them but the system can be very complicated and time-consuming and is not recommended unless you are desperate through lack of cash or perhaps wish to see how it works.

After taking your purchase to the usual till you may be told to proceed (or escorted if it is plain you are an English idiot!) to an Accounts Department in the far reaches of the establishment, often the top floor! There you will be led through a complicated procedure before eventually receiving your credit card voucher which you then take back to the till where you started − if you can remember where it is − to receive your parcel. Have a go if you fancy it and have plenty of time to spare − not if your parking meter is about to run out!

This might be a good place to mention that if you pay for your holiday or your ferry tickets using your Access card you are automatically given a certain amount of personal travel insurance. Worth thinking about before you pay by cash or cheque.

Further information

You will find lots of useful information about taking your money abroad in *Travel Money* by Wendy Elkington, also published by **Rosters Ltd.**

Personal documents

Passports and Visas: No visa is required for Germany but you will need a valid passport. An application form is available at any Post Office but remember that it can often take many weeks before your passport is ready.

33

A Visitor's passport, which is much cheaper but lasts for only one year, can be obtained while you wait at a main Post Office price £7.50 (or £11.25 for a husband and wife). You will need passport size photographs and some proof of identity.

Form E111: If you fall ill or have an accident you will be entitled to free medical treatment under a reciprocal arrangement between the British and German Health Services but only if you obtained a Form E111 from the Department of Social Security. These used to be valid for a limited time but are now for an indefinite period so you will only need to apply once — at least four weeks before you plan to travel abroad.

Car documents

If you are travelling in your own car, you will need a GB sticker — this will usually be supplied free by the ferry company or travel agent. And you should check that you have your Car Registration Document and your Drivers Licence. A "Green card" car insurance certificate is needed and is obtainable for an extra charge from your insurance company. It would also be wise to take out additional insurance in the form of AA 5 Star Cover or a similar package from another major motoring organisation or your own insurance company or travel agent.

Motor accessories

For driving in Germany you must have a red warning triangle and a first aid kit. Your headlamps must also be adjusted or partially blocked out so that they do not dazzle oncoming traffic on the other side of the road.

Clothes

Casual international clothing is worn almost everywhere though metropolitan Germans are very fashion conscious, particularly in *Munich* and *Hamburg* where long evening dresses and dinner jackets are sometimes worn when going to the opera.

You will need a raincoat and sunglasses at almost any time of the year as the weather can be unpredictable. Even in July and August, the hottest summer months, you might need a light sweater in the evenings. Comfortable walking shoes are a "must" almost everywhere as you will miss a lot if you are unable to get out into the countryside.

Electrical equipment
The voltage in Germany is 220V. Take an International Travel plug so that your hair dryer/travel iron or mini-boiler can be used safely.

CHAPTER FIVE:
COPING WITH THE LANGUAGE

Sprechen Sie Deutsch?

It is not true that "everybody in Germany speaks English". Although most of the younger people have learnt English at school, many of the older generation, particularly in the country areas, cannot understand it. It is of course perfectly possible to have an enjoyable holiday without speaking any German. One way to manage is by keeping to the main tourist centres where you can generally find someone who speaks English. But it is much more fun, and allows far greater scope, if you can manage just enough German to keep yourselves fed and housed or to make friends with the local population.

Time to learn?

A course of evening classes is usually available in most towns and these are fairly inexpensive and quite enjoyable. If there is not time for that, try your local library for language records — this will help to attune your ear to German pronunciation.

Take a phrase book

Buy a good phrase book. We swear by *Traveller's German*, one of a series of phrase books published by Pan. These little books fit into your pocket and are full of useful phrases and understandable phonetic help in pronunciation. We used this on our first visit when we spoke no German at all and found it indispensable.

For absolute beginners these very basic notes on the German language may also help.

Pronunciation

Generally speaking every letter in a German word is sounded. For example, the German word for a map is *Karte*. If it was an English word we would probably pronounce it as "cart". But in German, every letter, even the final "e", is sounded, so you would say "carter".

While almost every vowel and consonant differs in some way from English pronunciation, at a basic level you really need only bother with the following differences:

German J sounds like Y	eg *Jahre* (year)	= Yarrer
S	Z	*sieben* (seven)	= zeeben
V	F	*vier* (four)	= fear
W	V	*Wo?* (Where?)	= Vo?

Some letters have two dots over the top, called an *Umlaut*, which changes the sound of the vowel, and means that you must imagine that a letter "e" follows that vowel. For example, the word *schön* is pronounced "shern" rather than "shone".

Lots of capital letters and long words

Every noun begins with a capital letter, even in the middle of a sentence.

Germans love long words! All they do is join a number of words together. Whereas we would say "heavy weight championship", Germans say *Schwergewichtsmeisterschaft!* This can cause difficulties when you try to find the words in a dictionary as you may need to look up each part separately.

Numbers

Large numbers are difficult — particularly when a stallholder rattles off a long list of prices. Have your paper and pencil ready. Numbers up to ten are worth learning if you don't already know them.

0	*null* (nool)
1	*eins* (ines)
2	*zwei* (tsvy)
3	*drei* (dry)
4	*vier* (fear)
5	*fünf* (foonf)
6	*sechs* (zex)
7	*sieben* (zeeben)
8	*acht* (ahkt)
9	*neun* (noyn)
10	*zehn* (tsain)

The days of the week
(Stress first half of word)

Monday	*Montag* (mon-tahk)
Tuesday	*Dienstag* (deens-tahk)
Wednesday	*Mittwoch* (mitt-vok)
Thursday	*Donnerstag* (donners-tahk)
Friday	*Freitag* (fry-tahk)
Saturday	*Samstag or Sonnabend* (zams-tahk or zonn-ahbent)
Sunday	*Sonntag* (zonn-tahk)

Place names
You will already be familiar with the anglicized version of some important cities and other places in Germany. Some of the names have been changed almost completely, others just slightly. If you are not aware of the true German names you might find some signposting confusing, so here are a few "translations":

Cologne	*Köln*
Munich	*München*
Brunswick	*Braunschweig*
Hamelin	*Hameln*
Hanover	*Hannover*
Nuremberg	*Nürnberg*
Bavaria	*Bayern*
Moselle	*Mosel*
Rhine	*Rhein*
Danube	*Donau*
Lake Constance	*Bodensee*

Throughout this book, as in most guide books, the English versions have been used but when you are in Germany remember to use and look out for the proper names.

General conversation

Guten Morgen (Gooten Morgen)	Good morning
Guten Tag (Gooten Tak) . . .	Good day
Guten Abend (Gooten Abent)	Good evening
Auf Wiedersehen (Auf Veeder-zayn)	Good bye
Bitte (Bitter) . . .	Please
Danke (Danker) . . .	Thank you
Mein Nahme ist ___ (Mine Narmer ist ___)	My name is ___
Entschuldigen Sie bitte (Entshool-digen-zee bitter)	Excuse me please
Ich verstehe nicht (Ish fer-shtay-er nisht) . . .	I don't understand
Können Sie das aufschreiben? (Kernen Zee dass owf-shry-ben?) . . .	Can you write that down?
Ich spreche nicht Deutsch (Ish shpraysher nisht Doytsh)	I don't speak German

Shopping
Big shops and supermarkets are easiest, but in a smaller shop simply ask;
Wievel kostet dies?
   (Vee-feel kostet dees) . . .   What does this cost?

Restaurants
There is usually a menu on the table, but if not say:

Die Karte bitte
   (Dee carter bitter) . . .   The menu please

After your meal you will probably have to ask for the bill because they think it rude to offer it before you do. So say:

Die Rechnung bitte
   (Dee Recknung bitter) . . .   The bill please

Asking for a room
To start the conversation all you have to say is:

Haben Sie ein Zimmer frei?
   (Haben Zee ine Zimmer fry?)   Do you have a room
                               free?

And then add for how many nights:

- *für eine Nacht*
   (Foor eyner Nakt) . . .   for one night

— *für zwei Nächte*
   (foor zveye Nayshter) . . .   for two nights

They may reply:

*Ich habe keine Zimmer mehr
frei*
   (Ish hahbeh kyneh Zimmer
   mair fry) . . .   I have no rooms left

Es tut mir leid, wir sind
   ausgebucht
   (Ess toot meerlite veerzint
   owsgaybookt) . . .   Sorry, we're full

If they are not full and you would like to see the room (they will not mind being asked) say:

Kann ich mir das Zimmer
   ansehen?
   (Can ish meer dass Zimmer
   an zayen?) . . .   Can I see the room?

   And the price:

Wievel kostet es?
   (Veefeel kostet ess?) . . .   How much is it?

You may want to know what time breakfast is served:

Wann gibt es Frühstück?
   (Van geept es Froostook?)   What time is breakfast?

Use sign language, a pencil - and a smile

It is surprising what can be done with sign language and pencil and paper. For example, when you ask how much they are charging for the room, or the time for breakfast, you will probably not understand their answer at all, but if you ask them to write it down the problems will be overcome. You will find that you can manage with very little German but that any attempt to speak the language will be much appreciated — and, as in all parts of the world, a friendly smile can work wonders.

CHAPTER SIX:
GETTING AROUND IN GERMANY

Easy driving

The Germans have an excellent toll-free *Autobahn* system begun during the Nazi period but greatly expanded after the war. Today there are nearly 5000 miles of motorway and 20,000 miles of national highways of excellent quality. An *Autobahn* is indicated by an "A" on a blue sign. If it is part of the European network, it will also have a green "E" number, often a different number, which can lead to confusion. A national or regional road is designated by a "B" on a yellow sign. You will probably not wish to do all your travelling on the *Autobahn* — one motorway is, after all, much like any other — but the extensive network does mean that if you are short of time or need to get from one part of the country to another quickly there is almost always an accessible motorway which will cut hours off your journey.

Lane discipline

German drivers appear to be, on the whole, law-abiding and relatively sane. They are very lane-disciplined and will always move into a nearside lane to allow faster traffic to pass. If you are flashed it is because you are being inconsiderate and failing to leave the fast lane as soon as you can.

Speed limits

On the *Autobahn* the speed limit of 80mph is "advisory" and you will find that some of the traffic does travel very fast. The limit on four lane highways is 80mph (130kph) and on ordinary roads it is 60 mph (100kph) unless you are towing a caravan or trailer when the limit is 50mph (80kph). In built-up areas it is 30mph (50kph).

Rules of the road

● You must, of course, drive on the *right* side of the road.
● You have to give priority to the right unless otherwise indicated.
● Driving on side lights only is not allowed and dipped headlights are obligatory when visibility is poor and after sunset.
● Front *and* rear seat belts (if fitted) must be worn while travelling and children under 12 are not allowed to travel in the front seat of a vehicle fitted with rear seat belts.
● The maximum permitted blood/alcohol level is 80mg/100ml as in this country and there are increasing penalties if this level is exceeded.

Signposting

Motorway signposting is consistent and clear once you get the hang of it. Before an exit, *Ausfahrt*, you will see a large sign indicating the road number and its destination. The following sign will mention the next town for which there will be an exit and the ultimate destination of the motorway ahead. *Autobahnkreuz* (motorway junctions) where two motorways cross or merge can be nerve-racking for the navigator − not to mention the driver − and it is well worth while doing a bit of research ahead of time using the Autobahn Service leaflet obtainable from the German Tourist Office or motoring organisations.

Motorway rest areas

Those used to driving on British motorways will notice a welcome difference in the number of places to stop on the *Autobahn*. Every twenty or thirty miles there are *Raststätten* (rest stops) which are open 24 hours a day and where you may drink, eat or use the toilet facilities and sometimes find a bed for the night. In between these, every three miles or so on some motorways, you will find small rest stops where you can park, picnic or simply stretch your legs.

Breakdowns

If your car breaks down on the motorway you can call the breakdown services by using the orange telephones along the road. Ask for the *Strassenwachthilfe* (road service assistance). Help is given free of charge to members of affiliated organisations (such as the AA and RAC) and only parts have to be paid for. Black triangles on posts indicate the direction of the next telephone. You should put your red warning triangle 150 yards back towards the oncoming traffic.

Parking in towns

When visiting a town look out for the *Stadmitte* or *Zentrum* signs which indicate the way to the town centre. Parking in small towns and villages is usually free and seldom difficult. In larger towns you may need a parking disc, a blue clock card, to show your time of arrival. These can be obtained from garages, tourist offices or the police station. In the largest towns and busy holiday or tourist resorts you will probably have to pay to stop in a car park, *Parkplatz/Parkhaus*, or at a meter so make sure you have some small change for the machines.

Traffic lights, trams and pedestrians

You will find that traffic lights are sometimes placed over the traffic lanes. In towns, be careful when turning into another street at a junction. Pedestrians have priority crossing the road on their green light, which will probably be simultaneous with yours. German pedestrians are punctilious about waiting for the green light − remember this when you are walking round towns. You will be looked at askance if you cross just because the road is clear!

Also keep your eyes open for tram stops. The tram will

stop in the centre of the road and passengers will get off and on confident that the traffic will stop for them. Make sure you do!

Car ferries

Germany has some very large rivers cutting through some of the busiest and most attractive areas. These can be crossed by car ferries which are frequent and efficient and can cut miles off the trip to the next available bridge. The *Rhine* between *Koblenz* and *Mainz* is criss-crossed with ferries — fourteen for foot passengers and six for cars — and there are several across the *Mosel*.

At the mouth of the *Weser* there are at least four car ferries between *Bremerhaven* and *Bremen* and there are two on which you can take your car across the *Elbe* north of *Hamburg*. The *Danube* also has several ferries which cross between *Passau* and *Regensburg* and there is a service across *Lake Constance* between *Konstanz* and *Meersburg*.

Diversions

You may find the road unexpectedly blocked with a yellow sign with the word *Umleitung* pointing down a side road. *Umleitung* simply means "diversion" and, although it is obviously useful to have a map handy on these occasions, you can be certain that by following the *Umleitung* signs you will eventually be returned to the original road. Sometimes these diversions are very lengthy so don't be worried if you travel many miles before reverting to your route.

Incidentally, you may be interested to know that on the *Deutsche Reisekarte* maps (published by *Kümmerly + Frey*) the roads to be used in case of motorway closures are indicated by a blue line so if you know that a particular motorway section is under repair you can see in advance which way you will be advised to go. A far-sighted system which could be usefully adopted in this country.

Petrol stations

Petrol stations are frequently self-service, *Selbst tanken*, which makes things easier when you don't know how to ask for so many litres. Some petrol pumps are fitted with machines which produce a small bill showing the amount you have to pay. Look out for these or when you go into the office to pay you will be greeted by a long speech and a questioning look when you fail to produce the ticket. Unleaded, known as *Blei Frei*, is widely available.

Road signs

Road signs conform to the International system but some notices may need translation.

Achtung	Caution
Anlieger frei	Access to residents only
Ausfahrt	Exit from motorway
Autobahn	Motorway
Autobahnkreuz	Motorways merge
Bläue Zone	Restricted parking zone - disc needed
Durchfahrt verboten	No through traffic
Durchgangsverkehr	Through traffic
Einbahnstrasse	One-way street
Einfahrt	Entrance, start of motorway
Einfahrt Freihalten	Do not obstruct entrance
Einordnen	Get in lane
Ende (der Autobahn)	Motorway ends
Engstelle	Road narrows
Fahrspur Gesperrt	Lane closed
Fussgängerzone	Pedestrian precinct
Gefahr	Danger
Gefährliche Kurve	Dangerous bend
Gegenverkehr	Two-way traffic
Geschwindig-keitsgrenze	Speed limit

Grenzübergang	Frontier
Höchstge- *schwindigkeit*	Maximum speed
Hochgarage	Multi-storey car park
Hupen verboten	No sounding of horns
Kein Ausgang	No way out
Kein Durchfahrt	No thoroughfare
Keine Einfahrt	No access
Kein Eingang	Exit only, no entrance
Kein Zutritt	No entry
Krankenhaus	Hospital
Kreuzung	Crossroads
Kurvenreiche Strecke	Winding road
Langsam fahren	Drive slowly, slow down
Licht einschalten	Lights on
LKW	Lorries
Motor abstellen	Switch off engine
Nicht Überholen	No overtaking
Parken nur mit *parkscheiben*	Parking discs required
Parken verboten	No parking
Parkplatz	Car park
Parkzeit 30 minuten	Waiting limited to 30 minutes
PKW	Cars
Privatgrundstück	Private grounds
Radweg	Cycle path
Radweg Kreuz	Cycle crossing
Rastplatz	Lay-by
Raststatte	Services (on the motorway)
Rechts fahren	Keep right
Rollsplitt	Loose chippings
Rutschgefahr bei *nässe*	Slippery surface in wet weather
Sackgasse	Cul de sac
SB Tankstelle	Self-service petrol station
Schlechte Fahrbahn	Bad road surface
Selbst tanken	Self-service petrol

Seitenstreifen nicht Befahrbar	Soft verges
Stadtmitte	Town centre
Steinschlag	Falling stones
Strassenarbeiten	Roadworks
Strassenglätte	Slippery road surface
Tiefgarage	Underground car park
Überholen verboten	Overtaking forbidden
Umleitung	Diversion
Unbeschrankter Bahnübergang	Unguarded level crossing
Unfall	Accident
Verkehrsampeln	Traffic lights
Vorfahrt beachten	Give way: major road ahead
Zentrum	Town centre
Zoll	Customs

German Federal Railways

There is a complex and modern railway network throughout the country. Details of the main routes, facilities, timetables, fares and special tickets and offers can be found in a brochure **"Rail Travel Planner"** which you can get from the German National Tourist Office or from **German Federal Railways**. 10 Old Bond Street, London W1 Tel. (01) 499 0577.

Some special offers are only available in Germany but one which you can get from travel agents in this country is the **DB Tourist Card**. This allows travel on four, nine or sixteen consecutive days on the entire 17,400 mile network plus free travel on certain **Europabus** routes, reduced rates on **KD Rhine Steamers** and free entry to the *Nuremberg* railway museum.

There is also a *Tourenkarte* which gives ten days unlimited travel on rail services and 50% reduction on buses operated by German Railways on a regional basis for a given area such as the *Black Forest* or the *Central Rhineland* (there are 74 regions to choose from!) but this can only be obtained in Germany or in connection with a *DB* (German railway) tour. **Inter-rail** tickets are available to those under 26; **Tramper Monthly tickets** for those under 23 and students under 27; and those between 12 and 22 (or 26 for full-time students) are eligible for a **Junior Rail Pass**. For senior citizens there is a **Rail Europ Senior** ticket which offers considerable savings (up to 30%) for men over 65 and women over 60. It is available from British Rail travel centres and major railway stations.

Bus services

There are few long-distance bus services. *Europabus/ Deutsche Touring* run services on special scenic routes such as the Romantic Road and the Road of the Castles but other buses operated by Post or German Railways run mainly between small towns and villages especially those without railway stations.

Boat services

Regular scheduled boat services operate on most of the large rivers including the *Danube, Main, Mosel, Rhine, Neckar, Inn, Ilz* and *Weser* and also on lakes *Ammersee, Chiemsee, Königsee* and *Bodensee*. There is also a service in the *Kiel Fjord* and from *Cuxhaven* to *Helgoland* and the *East* and *North Frisian Islands*. Special excursion trips are also offered on all these navigable waters. On the *Danube* there are also international services to *Vienna* and *Linz* in Austria.

The *KD German Rhine Line* has 27 ships which operate daily on the *Rhine* and *Mosel* from Easter to October. Full information about their cruises and other services can be obtained from: *KD German Rhine Line, Frankenwerft 15, D-5000 Köln 1, West Germany.*

Urban services

Good public transport services exist in all towns. There are bus services in all urban areas supplemented by underground and suburban railway lines in a number of larger cities. It is often convenient to buy block tickets at a reduced rate to cover several journeys, or daily tickets giving unlimited travel are available. In big cities you will see ticket machines at boarding points and it is necessary to buy your ticket before you get on the train, bus or tram otherwise you risk a fine from the travelling inspectors. If you have bought a block of tickets you must cancel the one you are using by clipping it in a machine called *Entwerter* which you will find fixed near the entrance.

CHAPTER SEVEN: EATING

Very few visitors go to Germany just for the food but though *nouvelle cuisine* may be hard to find, good food is plentiful and eating and drinking seems to be a national occupation.

Breakfast

Probably the only meal you will have in your hotel or guesthouse will be breakfast, *Frühstück*, which is likely to consist of bread (sometimes black in Bavaria) or rolls and butter with a plate of cold meat and/or cheese slices and possibly jam. The waiter or waitress will ask you *"Möchten Sie Tee oder Kaffee?"* — to which you reply *"Tee bitte"* or *"Kaffee bitte"* as you prefer.

You will then be left to get on with your breakfast. Sometimes — and we have not yet worked out when this will happen and when it will not — a boiled egg will be on the table when you arrive or may turn up at any point in the meal. It will be fairly hard boiled, quite often hardly warm and sometimes with a cosy on it — even a straw bonnet!

In a larger hotel you may find a buffet-style meal where you will help yourself from an assortment of bread and rolls, sliced meat, cheese, jam, fruit etc.

Snacks

If you are in a hurry during the day, there are plenty of "fast-food" snack bars around. Look for a *Schnellimbiss, Imbisstube,* or a *Bratwurstand* (sausage stall) or a *Hähnchen-*

Grill (chicken takeaway). Or try the butchers' shops where you can often buy a roll filled with meat, ham or sausage. In addition to the local chains of *Wienerwald* (chicken takeaways) and *Nordsee* (fish restaurants), you will find MacDonalds in most large towns — useful for their toilets — but you will probably prefer to try the local food!

Try a supermarket

The hypermarket or supermarket restaurant is a good place to attempt your first meal out. Everything is labelled and priced and it is self-service so you can help yourself, or point, giving an opportunity to try something that looks enticing or different.

Lunchtime menus

Lunchtime is the cheapest time to eat in restaurants. You will quite often find a set menu, *Gedeck*, available. You may be horrified when you look at it. Words like *Schweinfleisch* (pork) and *Schinken* (ham), not to mention *Salzkartoffeln* (boiled potatoes), can be quite off-putting. And unless you are a gourmet you may prefer to avoid *Aufsnittmatzes* which seem to be pieces of raw fish!

Starters will be found under the heading of *Vorspeisen*, the most usually available being *Suppe* (soup). Fish dishes are listed under *Fischgerichte*, meat under *Fleischgerichte*, though chicken may come under *Gerflügelgerichte* and game *Wildgerichte*. Vegetables are known as *Gemüse*. German puddings, *Nachtische*, are generally confined to quite elaborate ice-creams or *Apfelstrudel*.

On any menu you will find several types of *Wurst* (sausage) and *Schnitzel* (pork or veal escalope), sometimes *Wienerschnitzel* (veal escalope in breadcrumbs) or cooked in other ways and with various sauces. Other meat dishes include *Deutsche Beefsteak* or *Hackbraten* which is a hamburger; *Rindfleisch* is beef; *Kalbfleisch* is veal and *Lamm* is lamb. Chops are *Koteletts* and steak is *Steak!* Anything starting with *Brat* is fried, *Rost* has been roasted and if it includes *Knödel* it has dumplings with it.

You will find your "Traveller's German" will help a lot but try just being brave and pointing to something and asking *"Was ist das?"* - "What is that?" The waiter will do his best to be helpful. They usually know the English names of food even if they are not able to hold a conversation with you.

Regional dishes

The dishes offered vary from region to region. Look out for some of these specialities on the menu *(die Speisekarte)*:

● **In Hesse**

Rippchen mit Sauerkraut	Ribs of pork with pickled cabbage
Zweibelkuchen	Onion-filled pastry
Frankfurter Kranz	Cream cake
Grüne Sosse	Green sauce made from seven herbs

● **In Westphalia and Northern Rhineland**

Reibekuchen	Potato pancakes
Pfefferpotthase	Spiced beef with bay leaves
Moselhecht	Mosel pike with cream and cheese

● **In Stuttgart and Baden Württemberg**

Schlachtplatte	Sauerkraut, liver sausage and boiled pork
Maultaschen	Ravioli
Spätzle	Noodles
Eingemachtes Kalbfleisch	Veal stew with white sauce and capers
Schwarzwälder Kirschtorte	Black Forest gateau

● In Munich and Bavaria

Leberkäs	Pork and beef paste
Spanferkel	Sucking pig
Weisswurst	White sausages
Leberknödelsuppe	Liver dumpling soup
Nürnberger	
Lebkuchen	Gingerbread
Rostbratwurst	Grilled sausages
Knödel	Dumpling stuffed with bacon
Steckerl Fisch	Spit-roasted fish
Schnitz und Speck	Stewed pears and apples with bacon

● In Hamburg and Northern Germany

Labskaus	Hotpot with fried eggs
Rote Grütze	Groats in fruit juice (delicious!)
Heidschnuckenbraten	Lüneberger Heath mutton
Bookweeten-	
Janhinnerk	Buckwheat pancake with bacon
Hamburger Aalsuppe	Soup of eel, dumplings, prunes, meat, peas
Birnen, Bohnen und	
Speck	Pears, beans and bacon

● In Bremen

Kohl und Pinkel	Cabbage and spare ribs
Matjes Hering	White herring
Hannoversiches	
Blindhuhn	Chicken hotpot

Afternoon tea

Mid-afternoon is the time to try a visit to a *Konditorei* for tea, or more usually coffee, and cakes. This is an expensive treat but one you will probably find difficult to resist if you are wandering round a small town or resort and see the mouth-watering array of *Kuchen* (cakes) and *Torte* (gateaux) in the windows of the coffee shops. The procedure is a little complicated. It is not usual just to go in and find a table. You first visit the counter of the shop and choose which cakes you prefer. You will be given a number (like a raffle ticket or the numbers used on the delicatessen counter in a British supermarket) and sometimes asked if you want it *mit Rahm* (with cream). You take your number with you and find a table in the café part of the premises. When the waitress comes to take your order for coffee or tea she will take your number with her and return with your chosen cake. You will find this indulgence will cost £4−5 for two but do try it at least once!

Evening meals

Evening meals are more difficult than lunches. The set menus seem to vanish and full scale meals from the à la carte menu can be rather more expensive. If you have eaten well at lunchtime and don't need much more, an *Abendbrot*, a plate of sliced meat, cheese and salad or a *Platte* (platter) of *Käse* (cheese) or *Wurst* (sausage) will probably be more than sufficient.

Asking for the bill

In most restaurants and bars you will have to ask for the bill − *"Zahlen bitte"* or *"Die Rechnung bitte"*. No-one will hurry you to leave even if you haven't ordered anything for the last hour or so and you could sit and wait for a long time before you realise that no bill is forthcoming. The bill will probably include a ten per cent service charge called *Bedienung* which makes up part of the wages of the waiter or waitress and is not, therefore, really a "tip", so it is usual to leave a few coins or the small change from your bill.

Self-catering

If you are self-catering, you can be as adventurous or as conservative as you wish. If you want your meals "just like at home", you will find most supermarkets and hypermarkets have familiar packets and tins. The fish, meat and delicatessen counters will probably tempt you to be brave and to try some of the dozens of different kinds of meat, sliced sausage, and regional cheeses. In a really small village you will have to patronize the local *Bäckerei* for bread and cakes, the *Metzgerei* or the *Schlächterei* for meat, sausages etc. and the *Obst-und-Gemüsehändler* for your fruit and vegetable. Point and hold up the required number of fingers and you will manage quite well — though maybe you had better not use this system for two!

CHAPTER EIGHT:
DRINKING

Which are more famous? German wines or German beers?
It's hard to say, but one thing is certain, they are famous
because they are good!

It is generally agreed that they are unique, and that no other
country has really managed to copy their style. One of the
main reasons for the Germans' success over the years has
been their insistence on high quality. And it is a fact that they
are very concerned that under European Community laws
they may soon be forced to accept imported beers which are
adulterated with chemicals.

Wines

Although Germany exports huge quantities of white wines,
you will have to search hard on shelves in Britain to find
many red ones. They do make red wine, but as Germany is
the northernmost major wine producer, it is not very easy for
them to do so except in a few places. Red wines generally
need long hot summers, and the cooler climes of Germany
cannot guarantee the warmth needed. But their white wines
are excellent and have a taste which is their own, different
from those of any other country.

Liebfraumilch — forget it!

Liebfraumilch can be found everywhere in Britain, from the
high street wine store, right down to the little grocer on the
corner. And it is very cheap. Don't knock *Liebfraumilch* —
there is nothing wrong with it and it would be hard to beat

as a pleasant and inexpensive wine. But ask for it in Germany and hardly anyone will know what you are talking about. *Liebfraumilch* is a name used on a very large scale to describe a fairly ordinary wine for export.

The average English restaurant is pretty unenterprising as far as German wines are concerned. You will find *Liebfraumilch* listed, also *Niersteiner Gutes Domtal* and *Piesporter*, but precious little else. In the supermarket you will come across Blue Nun and the like. But when you are in Germany, be more adventurous, and if you see a name you recognise, ignore it and try something else.

Quality laws

German wine is graded according to strict quality laws which are linked to the natural sugar content of the wine. If the level is low then sugar has to be added, and the quality grading is lower. The natural sugar content of the wine in its natural state depends very largely upon the weather. In a poor year the percentage of high quality wines drops markedly. The output of vineyards is subject to regular stringent testing and the quality level on the label can be relied upon.

The following official gradings are applied:

TAFELWEIN: Unless you are cooking, forget it. It is inexpensive, but far better wine can be bought almost as cheaply.

LANDWEIN: The wine is a little better than Tafelwein, but don't spend your money on it.

QUALITÄTSWEIN: This is the lowest level of "quality" wine and is certainly better than Tafelwein or Landwein. The word *Qualitätswein* will appear on the label. Most of the commonly available wines in the U.K. are ordinary *Qualitätswein*, such as, yes you've guessed, *Liebfraumilch, Niersteiner Gutes Domtal* and *Piesporter*. Nice enough to drink at home, but when you are on holiday why not have something better?

QUALITÄTSWEIN *MIT PRÄDIKAT*: These are the really good-quality wines. One of the rules for this category is that

NO sugar is allowed to be added at fermentation. The label will show the all-important additional words *"mit Prädikat"*. These *Qualitätswein mit Prädikat* levels of wine are further subdivided as follows:

KABINETT: Usually light and delicate, considered by many to be the nicest wines for ordinary drinking. They range from very dry (*Trocken*) to slightly sweet (*Halbtrocken*).

SPÄTLESE: These are more alcoholic, and are made from late-picked grapes, giving a usually fuller and sweeter drink.

AUSLESE: These are stronger, and are made from specially selected bunches of grapes. The taste is usually richer than *Kabinett* or *Spätlese* wines.

BEERENAUSLESE: We are now entering the exotic, as at this level the wine is made from individually selected over-ripe berries. As you would expect, *Beerenauslese* can be expensive.

TROCKENBEERENAUSLESE: You will probably never see this. It is very rare indeed, very expensive, and is made from single shrivelled over-ripe grapes.

You don't have to spend a lot of money to get a *mit Prädikat* wine, and you should have no trouble finding *Kabinett* level at a price which is very little above the great wine lake of ordinary *Qualitätswein*.

Wines in restaurants

In a German restaurant there will usually be a good selection of high-quality wines, but you can also order the 'house' wine. If you don't want a whole bottle, ask for "ein Viertel" and you will probably be given an empty glass together with a quarter-litre of wine in a small jug although in some places a large glass already filled will be given to you. It will not be a high quality wine, but it will be quite drinkable and the chances are that it will be very local. *Offener Wein* — from the barrel — is commonly available, especially in country areas.

Bringing wines back home

If you are thinking of bringing some wine back with you, consider these guidelines:

1. Try to buy only *mit Prädikat* wines. *Kabinett* level can be quite inexpensive although you may wish to try some of the dearer *Spätlese* or *Auslese* types.

2. Remember that if you buy the wines in Germany you will enjoy a much greater customs allowance than if you buy them on board ship or at a "duty free" shop.

3. Supermarkets are a good place to get your wines. Prices are lower, and you can look around the shelves without feeling pressured into buying. Visit a local vineyard by all means. This can be very interesting but don't imagine that you will come away with any great bargains.

4. Don't bother with non-German wines. They will tend to be about the same price as you would pay at home.

5. The green bottles will contain wines from the *Mosel-Saar-Ruwer* area, while the brown bottles are for the rest of Germany including the *Rhine*. In the higher price brackets, the experts tend to feel that the *Mosel* wines generally have the edge over other areas but it is very much a matter of personal opinion.

6. Make sure that the wine is "vintage". That doesn't have to mean expensive, but simply that the year of production is shown on the bottle. If a year is not shown the producer may have mixed wines from different years, the good with the less good.

7. Finally, if you want to find out more about wines, then buy some books on the subject. A recommended one is Hugh Johnson's Pocket Wine Book which comes out every year.

It really does slip into your pocket and contains a wealth of quickly accessible information which will help you identify almost every type of wine on the shelves.

Is it worthwhile bringing wine back from Germany? You will certainly save money because the shelf price of wine in Germany is lower than in Britain. You will also have the pleasure of drinking wines which cannot be bought over here. And over the months to come the opening of these bottles will be a reminder of your holiday.

German beer
Germans drink more beer per head of population than any other nation. The amazing thing is that they seem able to drink large quantities of beer during an evening and thoroughly enjoy themselves without spoiling things for everybody else. If you go to a beer hall or festival you are unlikely to come across any objectionable drunkenness — and if you do it will almost certainly be foreigners and not Germans. In these places you will probably be served beer in a large and very heavy glass mug which holds something like two pints. Some of the waitresses are able to carry ten of these full glasses in their two hands. Just how they manage to do so we have never fathomed out. Don't try it yourself!

Wide variety
There is a huge variety of beers in Germany, much of it bottled. If you want draught beer you will ask for *"Fassbier"*; this will be the local brew and will be some form of light ale of medium strength. If you want a large glass ask for *"ein grosses Bier"*, a small glass is *"ein kleines Bier"*.

So far as bottled beer is concerned *"helles Bier"* is a light beer, *"dunkles"* is a darker brew. If you want a really strong drink, something like 6% proof, ask for a *"Bockbier"*.

Schnapps
Germans are fond of drinking a colourless spirit such as *Schnapps* or *Korn* with their beer. They down the spirit in

one go and then follow it up — more slowly — with the beer.
It is an idea you might like to try.

Drinking out

In most bars you sit at a table and wait to be served. But
don't scribble on the beer mat, as waitresses sometimes make
a pencil tick on the mat for every drink you have, totting it
all up at the end. Scribbling extra marks could cost you
dearly. You are not normally expected to pay as you go.
When you are ready to leave you will have to ask the waitress
for the bill (*"die Rechnung bitte"*, or *"Zahlen bitte"*). You can
sit there all evening without being pressed to buy more
drinks, unless of course you are in a busy city bar and seating
is at a premium.

In many pubs and bars there will be tablecloths on most
of the tables, but you will often see one large table near the
bar counter without a cloth. This table may, or may not, be
marked with the sign *Stammtisch*. Do not sit there as this will
be the table reserved for the local "regulars", and strangers
are not welcomed unless specially invited!

Don't drink and drive

You will find that the Germans make very fine wine and
excellent beer, and these help to make an enjoyable evening.
But remember that they are very strict about drinking and
driving in Germany, and the last thing you want on holiday
is to get involved with the police. So restrict your drinking
to a time when you have put the car away for the evening.
Zum Wohl!

CHAPTER NINE:
USEFUL INFORMATION

Time

Germany keeps to Central European time (MEZ) which means it is an hour ahead of Greenwich Mean Time in winter, but in summer (from the last Sunday in March to the last Sunday in October) it is two hours ahead of Britain.

Opening hours

Shops: Most shops are open from 9 or 9.30am to 6 or 6.30pm. Small shops such as bakeries, fruit and vegetable shops or butchers may open as early as 7am but often close for a couple of hours at noon, re-opening at 2pm or 3pm. Generally shops are closed on Sundays and on most Saturday afternoons.

Offices: Business hours are normally 8am to 5.30pm though Government offices are usually open to the public only in the mornings.

Banks: Banking hours are Monday to Friday 8.30 or 9am to 12 noon and after lunch from 1.30pm to 3.30pm, or 2.00pm to 4pm. In most towns, banks are also open on Thursdays until 5.30pm.

Rest days: On some shops and many small hotels and *Gasthöfe* you may see a sign *Ruhetag* . . . This indicates which day of the week is a "rest day", ie which day the establishment is closed. It is not usual for everywhere in a particular town to have the same closing day so if one place is shut you are likely to find somewhere else suitable open.

Customs

There are no restrictions on the amount of currency (German or foreign) that you can take into Germany at present. You are also allowed to take any reasonable amount of personal belongings or equipment and food for your own consumption. As an EEC citizen you are permitted to import the normal Customs' allowances of tobacco, alcohol etc duty free.

Health

No vaccination certificates are needed – except from travellers arriving from an infected area. Visitors from the UK are entitled to use the German health service and if you have brought your Form E111 (see Chapter Four) treatment will be free although you will be charged for prescribed medicines. There are also over 250 officially recognized spas and watering places offering various therapeutic treatments.

Keeping in touch

Telephones: Using the telephone in Germany is not too complicated. In the yellow public pay phones you need two 10 *Pfennig* coins to make local calls. For long distance calls you can either go to a Post Office *(Postamt)* where the operator will make the connection for you or you can use a public phone box with a green *Inland-Ausland* sign and dial direct. Make sure you have enough 1, 2 and *5DM* coins with you! Calls made from an hotel will be more expensive, generally about 60 *Pf* a unit. To contact the UK, you dial 0044 followed by the UK area code (leaving off the initial 0) and then the number you require. If you have any language difficulties you can always dial 00118 which will connect you to International Directory Enquiries.

Post Offices: These are usually open from 8am to 6pm with the smaller ones closing from 12−3pm for lunch. Those with a "ec" sign will cash your Eurocheques or Travellers cheques as well as Postcheques. If you leave home without a definite address you can arrange to have mail delivered to a named Post Office marked *Poste Restante*. You then call and collect it at the counter marked *Postlagernde Sendungen*.

Posting letters: The postal rate for letters both within Germany and to other EEC countries including Great Britain, is 80 *Pfennigs* (up to 20 grammes), 60 *Pfennigs* for postcards. The local mail boxes, *Brief-Kastern*, are emptied in the mornings and evenings, some are emptied more frequently. There is only a daily service on Saturdays.

When writing to an address in Germany you will notice that the postcode comes immediately before the place name eg *8000 Munich*.

Climate

Most of Germany is in the continental climate zone and can be really hot in the summer and bitterly cold in the winter. There is quite a difference between the northwest and the southeast. The North (around *Hamburg*) has less seasonal variation with milder winters and moderately warm summers.

If your visit is in the summer you are unlikely to be disappointed in the weather as German summers are generally hot and dry. The mountainous parts of Bavaria can have almost double the rainfall of the north of Germany.

You could have an enjoyable "summer" holiday anytime between late May to early October while those who like to ski could go from mid-December to March. We travelled to *Cologne* in early February to see the Rose Monday Carnival (a variation on the Mardi Gras celebrations in other countries) and found the temperature minus 13° Centigrade but crisp and dry and not too uncomfortable. But we were warmly dressed and had plenty of *Glühwein* available!

Public conveniences

Whether in town centres or in shops or restaurants etc. toilets are always clean and well cared for and with modern fitments and plumbing. The doors are marked with appropriate pictures to differentiate between "Ladies" and "Gentlemen" or look for the words *Damen* for ladies and *Herren* for gentlemen. In some country areas you may still find the symbol *00* on the door where there is just one toilet.

Tipping

Service charges and taxes are always included in hotel and restaurant bills. While it is not obligatory to leave an additional tip it is customary to leave some small change. It is usual to tip taxi drivers, hairdressers and cloakroom attendants.

Shopping

Almost all large and small towns have pedestrianised traffic-free shopping precincts where you can stroll undisturbed and there are often markets which are always interesting and fun to explore. There are several chains of supermarkets and department stores in town centres and some of these also have large out-of-town stores *(Einkaufzentrum)* where you can do almost all your shopping under one roof.

As far as serious shopping is concerned, specialities which are worth considering (if you can afford it!) are porcelain, silver, leatherware, tablelinen, *Solingen* knives, clocks from the *Triberg* region of the Black Forest, toys from *Nuremberg* and handmade crystal and glass of all kinds from the area around *Zwiesel* in *East Bavaria*.

You will also enjoy selecting your full allowance of wine and beer which are both excellent quality and value. You can, if you wish, bring back more than your customs allowance provided you declare it on arrival in the UK and pay the duty. If it is simply for your own enjoyment you will probably feel it is worth while even with the cost of the duty included. (And the "red" channel is often less busy than the green so you may save time as well!)

Nightlife

Generous subsidies mean that all large towns and cities, and many smaller ones, have their own theatre, opera house, orchestra and sometimes even a ballet company. There are also nightclubs, bars with live music and discos to suit every taste. In rural areas visitors are invited to traditional folk dances and musical evenings usually in local hotels. Many spa towns have a casino where the favourite games are roulette and baccarat. They are licensed and gambling is legal. Other places where casinos can also be found include *Wiesbaden, Travemünde* on the Baltic coast, *Konstanz* and *Lindau* on *Lake Constance*.

Drei drinks!

Sometimes ordering drinks can be tricky. On a recent trip we were in a motorway services cafe having a quick coffee when a coachload of British tourists were having difficulties. One of the party had asked for a "dry martini" but the waiter brought *three* glasses of vermouth. The German waiter could not understand what was wrong. He was quite sure they had ordered *drei* − three − martinis!

Wanderweg

In many parts of Germany, particularly in *Bavaria* and the *Black Forest*, you will find well-marked footpaths of various lengths. At the beginning of a walk you will usually find a *Wanderparkplatz*, a car park where you may leave your car free of charge while you are enjoying your walk. The local tourist office will be able to give you details of walks in the area. In addition to ordinary footpaths, National Park areas have nature trails and some small towns also have special keep-fit trails with a series of exercise points provided with obstacles and apparatus which you have to negotiate on your way.

Formal behaviour

Manners are sometimes rather more formal than in this country. For instance, when you come down to breakfast in an hotel or *Gasthof* it is usual to greet everyone in the room with a *Guten Morgen* (Good morning) or, in the south, *Grüss Gott* (Greetings). You may even find that on entering a small restaurant, Germans will greet all the other diners with *"Guten Tag"* (Good-day) or *"Guten Abend"* (Good evening).

People shake hands on meeting and departing. If you are invited to someone's home it is customary to be on time and to take unwrapped flowers to the hostess, traditionally an uneven number. (Be careful about red roses — they are considered a lover's gift.)

The way of life

You will probably find that, in general, life in Germany is very similar to that in Britain. The lifestyle in France has noticeable differences but the Germans are much more like us in many ways. Nevertheless, don't expect everything to be the same — there would be little point in holidaying "abroad" if it were! Noticing the little differences will make your holiday more interesting. Look out for:

— small trees tied to the apex of roofs of new houses being built, left over from a kind of "topping-out" ceremony held by the builders.

— spare toilet rolls covered with decorated woolly "hats" carried on the back shelves of cars.

— parades by the local *Schützenverein*, the shooting club. In small country towns these are very popular with their banners, uniforms and ceremonials.

CHAPTER TEN:
FESTIVALS AND SPECIAL EVENTS

Folk and Wine Festivals

Festivals are an important part of life in Germany. If you are thinking of making a holiday trip you might wish to consider arranging your visit to coincide with a festival. Some of the specialist holiday companies can make all the arrangements for you if you prefer not to "do-it-yourself". Actual dates can vary from year to year so it would be wise to consult the German National Tourist Office who will provide an up to date list of events for any particular month or year. These are some of the most important regular festivals throughout the year.

January

Baden-Württemberg and Bavaria. Three Kings' Day, *Dreikönigstag*, is celebrated.

The Rhineland, Baden-Württemberg, Bavaria, Hesse etc. During the winter months, carnival events include masked balls, fancy dress parties and other festivities.

Bonn and Cologne. In early January there is a special event to proclaim the Carnival King.

Bremen. A traditional folk festival called the *Bremer* Eiswette.

Munich. The Carnival celebrations called *Fasching* are held in January and early February. **DER Travel Service** will take you there by rail or air.

February

Cologne, Bonn and other Rhineland towns. Parties continue until just before the beginning of Lent when the carnival proper begins with the *Weiberfastnacht*, the Women's Carnival Day held on the Thursday before Ash Wednesday. From early morning the streets are full of women in fancy dress going to the office, to work or to the shops. The Sunday before Lent is Children's Carnival Day when there is a procession of local school children in fancy dress through the city centre. Some suburban centres have their main procession on this day too, presumably so that everyone can go into town for the big event the next day. This is *Rosenmontag* (Rose Monday), the highlight of Carnival when an enormously long parade organised by the Festival Clubs winds its way around the city. There are hundreds of decorated floats from which brightly dressed people throw sweets and other goodies to the crowd. Stilt walkers, dozens of bands, groups of friends or club members in fancy dress, all cheered and clapped by the watching crowd very many of whom are themselves in fancy dress and in the mood to dance and sing.

Several companies run trips to Carnival. They include:

Applegates Supreme Coaches
B and H Travel Services Ltd
Bluebird Coaches
Central Liner, West Midlands Travel Ltd
H.E. Craiggs-Wansbeck Coaches
DER Travel Service
Woods Coaches Limited

March

Hamburg. "Dom", a folk festival.

Bavaria. Some Bavarian towns have an equestrian procession as part of their Whit festivities. A famous one held in the Bavarian Forest region is the *Kötztinger Pfingstritt* when about 500 beautifully dressed horses and riders process seven miles down the valley to a service held in a field.

April

Koblenz. A Wine and Flower Festival

Mannheim. The May Amusements Fair.

The Harz. Special festivities for Walpurgis Night.

Munich. The first *"Auer Dult"* of the year. Also held in July and August, this is an open air antiques and flea market with fairground amusements.

May

Bonn. A Spring version of 'The Rhine in Flames" followed by a Wine Festival.

Frankfurt. A folk festival called *"Waldchestag"*.

June

Eltville. A Wine and Flower Festival in mid-June.

Saarbrücken and Koblenz. Old Town Festivals are held in both towns.

Würzburg. The Annual Mozart Festival.

Landshut. A famous historical event is celebrated every four years (next in 1993). One of the greatest folk festivals in Europe it is held to commemorate the wedding of the daughter of the King of Poland to the son of Ludwig, Duke of Bavaria in 1475. "Wedding guests" wearing period costumes walk through the town to meet "Ludwig" who rides in a sedan chair and "Hedwig" in a golden bridal coach drawn by white horses and escorted by knights and jesters.

July

Dinkelsbühl. The *"Kinderzeche"* or children's festival is held. This commemorates the time in 1632 when a siege of the town was relieved as children carrying flowers marched out of the gates towards the enemy so softening their hearts and saving the town. Today's celebrations include performances of a play recalling these events as well as a folk festival with sword dancing and traditional music.

Ulm. In the middle of the month there is a Folk Festival which includes a procession on the river *Danube*.

Düsseldorf. The Rhine Fair.

Hamburg. International Musical Parade and a *"Hummelfest"* folk festival.

Mannheim. The Palitinate Folk Festival includes a grand firework display.

Kulmbach. "Beer Week".

Garmisch-Partenkirchen. The local festival.

Waldmünchen. Weekly open-air performances of a play *"Trenck der Pandour vor Waldmünchen"* which includes spectacular wild riding scenes recalling the occupation of the town during the eighteenth century by a Baron Trenck and his mounted soldiers known as Pandours.

August

Rüdesheim on the Rhine. Wine Festival.

Cochem and Winnigen on the Mosel. Wine Festival.

Nahe Valley towns. Wine Festivals.

Mainz. Wine Fair with a folk festival.

Bernkastel Kues. Wine Fair finishing with a firework display and a festival procession.

Many of these wine festivals can be visited as part of a coach trip. A list of companies offering tours is in Chapter Twenty.

Waldmünchen. Further performances of the *"Trenck der Pandour"*.

Koblenz. One of "The Rhine in Flames" celebrations. **Jay Tours Travel, Rules Coaches Limited** and **Shelton Orsborn** arrange holidays to include these festivities.

Straubing. The *Gäuboden* Folk Festival. See Chapter Thirteen.

Fürth im Wald. The *"Dragonstich"*. See Chapter Thirteen.

September

Lübeck. The Old Town Festival includes the *"Maritimer Meile"* held in the *Holstein Harbour*.

Oberwesel. A Wine Fair and the Night of 1000 Fires.

Bad Durkheim. The annual Sausage Fair and Wine Festival.

Koblenz. *"Schängelmarkt"* folk festival.

Neustadt/Weinstrasse, Grünstadt/Palitinate. Wine Festivals

Würzburg. The Vintners' Festival.

St. Goar/St. Goarhausen and Boppard. The main "Rhine in Flames" events. Visits can be arranged by **Angela Holidays or Cosmos Tours**.

Munich. The *Oktoberfest* begins in September and lasts until the first Sunday in October. Over 200,000 gallons of beer are drunk during the last weekend in September. In the opening procession, horse drawn beer drays join carnival tableaux on decorated floats in a parade through the streets to the festival grounds, the Lord Mayor taps the first barrel and a cannonade proclaims the news that the festival has begun. For many, it begins hours earlier as they dress in their fancy costumes or get up early to find a seat in the stands to watch the procession. The festival lasts for sixteen days finishing with another procession. In between there is the serious business of drinking in the numerous beer cellars and beer tents for the thousands of revellers while children can enjoy the amusements of the enormous fun-fair. If you fancy joining in **Dopple M European, DER Travel Service, Cosmos Tours** or **Vision Travel** arrange trips.

October
Boppard. Wine Festivals and fireworks.

Landau. The *"Fest des Federweissen"*.

Bremen. A folk festival with a procession.

November
Hamburg. Another "Dom" festival.

Winnigen and Trier on the Mosel. Wine festivals.

Hamburg, Lübeck, Frankfurt and Bonn. The Christmas Fairs begin.

December
Nuremberg. The *Christkindlmarkt*, the most famous of the Christmas Fairs, begins and lasts until the day before Christmas Eve. Trips can be booked through **Applegate Supreme Coaches** or **DER**.

Major trade fairs and exhibitions
Fairs and conventions of many important industries are held annually in German cities. You might wish to fit in a few days holiday around some of these events. There are several firms who will make arrangements for you including:

MGP (Special Event Travel)
Business and Trade Fair Travel Limited
EXPO Travel Services Limited
Ian Allen Travel Limited
IEL Travel Limited
LEP Fairs
LIMO (LEP International Meeting Organisers Limited)
Party and Business Travel Limited
VIP Travel Limited

January
Frankfurt. The International Trade Fair for Home and Household Textiles.

Düsseldorf. The International Boat Show.

February
Nuremberg. The International Toy Fair.

Munich. The International Trade Fair for clocks, watches, jewellery, precious stones and silverware.

Frankfurt. The International Fair — a consumer goods exhibition.

March
Hanover. The World Centre for Office, Information and Communications Technology.

Hamburg. The International Exhibition for the Hotel, Restaurant, Communal Catering, Bakery and Confectionery trades.

May, June and July
Frankfurt. The Federal German Horticultural Show.

August
Offenbach. The International Leather Goods Fair.

September
Cologne. The International Trade Fair for Sports Goods, Camping Equipment and Garden Furniture.

Frankfurt. The International Motor Show.

October
Frankfurt. The Book Fair.

November
Pirmasens. International Leather Week.

Sporting events

Many of these vary from year to year. Some annual events include:

Garmisch-Partenkirchen. International Winter Sports week.

Kiel. International Sailing Regatta (usually held during June).

Höckenheim. The German Grand Prix (usually at the end of July).

Hamburg. The German Open Tennis Championships (in April or May).

Several specialist travel firms will arrange visits to sporting occasions. If there is something you wish to see you could get in touch with:

Sports Spectator International Limited
Chequers Travel Limited

If you are taking part you could try:

Sportsmans Travel Limited

For visits to motor sport events such as the *Rallye Deutschland* or the German Grand Prix at *Höckenheim* and the 24 hour 1000km event at *Nürburgring* the specialist company is **Onspec Tours**.

Cultural and theatrical events

The list of musical and cultural events held in Germany is long and varied. Some are annual events, others take place at longer regular intervals, many are one-off special events. A full list of events taking place during any particular period or year can be obtained from the German National Tourist Office but here are just a few.

Bayreuth. One of the most important musical annual events is the *Bayreuth* Festival held each summer (usually starting towards the end of July and continuing through August) to

celebrate the music of Richard Wagner. **G.W. Henebery Limited** or **Heritage Travel** arrange visits.

Munich. The Opera Festival is in July and August. Trips are arranged by **Prospect Music and Arts Limited**.

Würzburg. The Mozart Festival is held in June. **Heritage Travel** arrange visits with air or coach travel.

Oberammergau. The most famous theatrical event is held only every ten years (those years ending in a 0). The *Oberammergau Passion Play* is performed during the summer months from mid-May to the end of September (for more details see Chapter Sixteen).

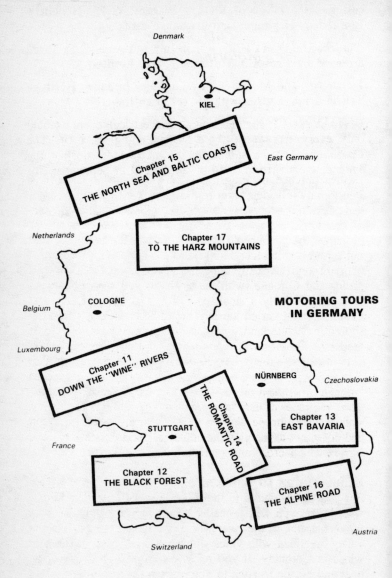

Denmark

KIEL

East Germany

Chapter 15
THE NORTH SEA AND BALTIC COASTS

Netherlands

Chapter 17
TO THE HARZ MOUNTAINS

Belgium

COLOGNE

**MOTORING TOURS
IN GERMANY**

Luxembourg

Chapter 11
DOWN THE "WINE" RIVERS

NÜRNBERG

Czechoslovakia

Chapter 14
THE ROMANTIC ROAD

Chapter 13
EAST BAVARIA

STUTTGART

France

Chapter 12
THE BLACK FOREST

Chapter 16
THE ALPINE ROAD

Austria

Switzerland

Part Two:
Motoring Tours

CHAPTER ELEVEN:
DOWN THE "WINE" RIVERS – THE RHINE AND MOSEL

Castles perched on crags, famous vineyards on incredibly steep sunny hillsides, river traffic of all kinds, historic towns and romantic scenery – no wonder the *Rhine* is rated as one of the world's greatest attractions, and cruising down it is probably the favourite German holiday. The *Rhine* is 820 miles long – the second longest river in Europe – 542 miles of it through Germany. The most famous section, between *Mainz* and *Cologne*, with its fortresses and scenery famous in legend, is only a small part of this great river. A most interesting and varied journey would be to follow it from its source in Switzerland, into and out of *Lake Constance*, past the *Rhine Falls* near *Schaffhausen*, then following the border with Switzerland as far as *Basel* and with France to *Karlsruhe*. It is then entirely in Germany until it reaches Holland at *Arnhem* on its way to the North Sea near *Rotterdam*. 552 miles of the *Rhine* are navigable and it is the busiest waterway in Europe with up to 9000 cargo-vessels going up and down not to mention the countless pleasure steamers and ferries which cross and recross.

From Mainz to Koblenz

For your introduction to the *Rhine*, particularly if you are a wine-lover, you will probably decide to start with the most famous stretch of the river where the hills at the sides of the valley are lined with vines which produce some of the best wines in Germany. If you resist the temptation to travel by boat and decide to stick to your car you can follow the B42 road from *Wiesbaden* on the west bank of the river. This road is called the *Rheingauer Riesling Route* and follows the river as far as *Koblenz* through famous vine-growing areas.

Your first stop down river will probably be *Eltville*, famous for its sparkling wine cellars, where they have a well-used and attractive promenade.

Rüdesheim

Rüdesheim, the next stop, is the favourite destination of *Rhine* visitors from all over the world and it is — as one guide book puts it — "very well organised to cater for the needs of its visitors". In other words it is very touristy and though admittedly attractive with its half-timbered houses and *Weinstuben*, it is often very crowded, particularly in the famous *Drosselgasse*, the narrow main street. Get away from the crush and wander off into the narrow lanes and side streets. If you have difficulty in parking or you simply cannot face the crowds, do not despair — there will be many more towns and villages just as attractive if not as famous!

Bingener Loch

From *Rüdesheim*, the next town is *Bingen* on the other side of the river, an important wine-centre and busy river-port where the *Nahe* joins the *Rhine* which now turns north through a narrow passage known as the *Bingener Loch*.

Castles and legends

This next sixteen-mile stretch of the river has been written about in prose, poetry and legend more than any other. The river is bordered by steep hills and rockfaces over which are dotted dozens of castles and castle ruins. Although perched on seemingly impregnable vertical crags, they have all been attacked and often destroyed in successive campaigns as possession of a strategically located castle allowed the owner to gather lucrative tolls from the river traffic.

You will pass *Ehrenfels* castle on the west bank while opposite, on the east bank, you will get a good view of *Rheinstein*, followed after the village of *Assmannshausen*, by

Drachenstein and then *Sooneck*. You can visit these if you wish by crossing the river by the ferry in *Assmannshausen*.

Bacharach

You may well choose to stay on the east bank as far as *Bacharach*, an attractive village and wine centre with medieval town walls round which you can stroll, looking down on – and I must confess sometimes into – the half-timbered houses in the narrow streets.

A little way south is the *Fürstenburg* castle while above the town is the *Stahleck* – once a fortress but now a youth hostel. Just below the *Stahleck*, we stayed some years ago in a small hotel, the *Weinhaus Blüchertal*, with a tiny water-tank type swimming pool in the courtyard. Having arrived after a long very hot drive, the pool and the cool pleasant hotel were indeed welcome.

Pfalz Grafenstein

A little further up river you will need to get your camera ready for one of the most photographed sights – the island of *Pfalz Grafenstein* where there was once a famous customs house from which a chain was strung across the river and only lifted when the boats had paid their dues.

Oberwesel

Next you will see the ruins of the *Schönberg* towering above *Oberwesel*, which describes itself as a "town of wine and towers". This small town was originally ringed by walls, with 21 towers of which 18 still survive, around the half-timbered houses and historic churches.

The Loreley

Soon it is cameras at the ready again for the Seven Virgins – seven partly submerged rocks which, according to legend, were maidens turned to stone on account of their prudishness. Then the *Loreley*, actually a rugged 435 foot high rock – but in the imagination of the famous German poet, *Heinrich Heine*, a seductive blonde mermaid who lured innumerable ships and boatmen by her singing and her beauty. Indeed the river at this point narrows through a gorge with submerged rocks needing the full attention of pilots of ships passing through. There are parking places here where you will find tourist stalls selling souvenirs, maps of the Rhine etc. to the coachloads of sightseers who stop at this point.

Burg Katz and Burg Maus

A short while after passing the *Loreley* you will see three fortresses at *St. Goarhausen* and, opposite, *St. Goar*. The castles, *Burg Katz* and *Burg Maus*, are on the west bank and *Burg Rheinfels* is above *St. Goar* on the eastern side.

The Rhine in Flames

In September, these two small towns are the centre of the spectacle known as *"The Rhine in Flames"* when each evening thousands of torches are lit along the sides of the river. The castles are illuminated with floodlights and there is a fantastic display of fireworks.

Boppard

Soon you will arrive at *Boppard*, the central point of this largest wine-growing region of the *Middle Rhine*. *Boppard* has a long promenade by the river and a cable car which, from March to October, will take you 990 feet up to the *Gedeons-Eck* where there is a magnificent view. If you are feeling energetic a 30-minute walk will take you to *Vier-Seen Blick* (Four Lake View) a superb vantage point where the river far below looks like a series of lakes.

The Lahn Valley

If you carry on along the west bank, you will arrive at *Lahnstein* where the river *Lahn* joins the *Rhine*. The *Lahn* valley with its wooded banks, ruined castles and delightfully situated small towns is well worth a detour if you have the time and the inclination. It is described in more detail in Chapter Thirteen.

Koblenz

Shortly after leaving *Lahnstein* you will see the first bridge crossing since you left *Mainz* and you will know you have reached *Koblenz* where the *Mosel* (this is the German spelling – unlike the French, they put the emphasis on the first syllable) joins the *Rhine* at the *Deutsches Eck* or German Corner.

The Mosel

The *Mosel* valley is, of course, of particular interest to wine lovers for whom the local tourist boards organize tours and visits to vineyards and cellars. It is even possible to spend your holiday in a vintner's house or enjoy fishing in the river. If you are interested enquire at the tourist office.

Like the *Rhine*, the *Mosel* has roads on both sides for much of its length and you can choose which you prefer. If you are driving out of *Koblenz* on the B416 you will first come to *Winnigen* and then *Kobern-Gondorf* where the road goes twice through a vast fifteenth to seventeenth century castle. A favourite tourist sight is *Burg Eltz*, a fortress situated in an awe-inspiring position above the *Eltz* river, three miles north of *Moselkern* station. A picture of *Eltz* castle appears on every *DM* 500 note.

Soon, at *Treis-Karden*, the 416 comes to an end and the road becomes the B49, known as the *Mosel Weinstrasse*. At *Cochem*, about 8 miles further on, there is a *Moselpromenade* with many cafés and inns where you can sit and enjoy the beautiful view across the river. A little further and you will come to *Beilstein*, an unspoiled village where some of the episodes of the popular German film *"Heimat"* were made. At *Marienburg*, the road goes through the deepest part of the valley as the river cuts through the limestone of the *Zell* bend and on through *Traben Trarbach* which, in addition to marvellous wines, has thermal springs and an annual international motorboat race.

Bernkastel-Kues

Like *Traben Trarbach*, this is actually two towns built one each side of the river, situated in the heart of the middle *Mosel Valley* and surrounded by one magnificent vineyard after another. *Bernkastel* has a renowned "romantic" marketplace, a seventh century castle, many half-timbered houses with elaborate weather vanes and the *Zentralkellerei* in which are stored 65 million litres of wine made by the 5,000 vintners in the area.

To Trier

From *Bernkastel* you continue on a journey through vineyards and wine villages − the oldest wine growing area in Germany where wines have been grown since Roman times − to *Trier*, Germany's oldest town which was founded by the Emperor Augustus in 16BC. There are many antiquities to be seen including the world-famous *Porte Nigra* built in the second century as a fortified Roman gateway. It is 36m wide, 30m high and is the biggest and best preserved north of the Alps. The *Hauptmarkt* is impressive and picturesque with its architecture ranging from Gothic to Renaissance and Rococo. Not far away, the birthplace of Karl Marx, at *Brückenstrasse* 10, is now a museum.

Koblenz to Cologne

Carrying on up the *Rhine* after, or instead of, the detour along the *Mosel*, finds us back in *Koblenz*. The junction of the two rivers here is bustling with steamers, barges, tugs and every other kind of river traffic and the promenade along the river is a popular walk and meeting place. The road along the west bank of the *Rhine* becomes Autobahn 9 from here to *Andernach*, a small town with an old quarter within ramparts and gates as well as a new viaduct built to carry the motorway north of the town. The valley narrows on its way to *Bad Breisig* via *Rheineck*, a castle which can be reached by a chair lift and which provides a good viewpoint. After the next town, *Sinzig*, where there is a thirteenth century church with Gothic vaulting, the lovely valley of the *Ahr* leads off west towards the *Eifel Massif*. The A9 goes on to *Remagen* where the railway bridge across the *Rhine* became famous in the annals of World War II.

Bonn

Soon the *Rhine* banks become lined with buildings as the outskirts of *Bad Godesberg* appear. This area serves as a suburb of *Bonn*, the capital city of the Federal Republic, and provides a pleasant setting for embassies, diplomatic missions, ministries and the offices of international organisations. There is a promenade along the river which is a popular place for a stroll especially in the evening. There is an excellent view of the *Siebengebirge*, the Seven Mountains, a range of wooded hills famous in legend. On the top of the *Drachenfels* are the ruins of an old castle which can be reached on foot or by an old cog-wheeled railway built in 1883. At the foot of the hills opposite *Bad Godesberg* is *Königswinter*, a busy tourist centre with flower-bordered walks and plenty of hotels which are rather cheaper than those in *Bonn* itself.

Previously a small university and historic town, *Bonn* was pitched into the limelight after World War II when it became the Federal Capital. Although many people, including some Germans, still think of *Berlin* as Germany's capital, *Bonn* is now the seat of government and the meeting place of the *Bundestag*, the Federal Parliament. It also houses most of the ministries and other official buildings. The new *Bonn* now incorporates *Bad Godesberg* and *Beuel* on the other bank of the river.

Bonn has 2000 years of history. A strategic town in Roman times, it became an important city in the thirteenth century when the Electors of Cologne moved there. They built a palace — now the home of the university — and laid out beautiful parks and avenues. Beethoven lived here and his birthplace is now a museum which contains personal mementoes, some of his musical instruments and original scores.

Home from Cologne

From *Bonn* or from *Cologne*, which is a little further down the river and is described in Chapter Eighteen, you can set off on a river trip on the *Rhine*, or visit the peaceful *Eifel* region. You can test your driving skills on the *Nürburgring*, go skiing among the hills of the *Sauerland*, or make business contacts in the commercial and industrial areas of the *Ruhr*. Or you can make your way home if your visit to Germany is at an end.

CHAPTER TWELVE:
TO THE BLACK FOREST

Mountains rising to nearly 4000 feet above picture-postcard valleys, welcoming spa towns, a variety of peaceful activities and wildlife − for many years tourists have enjoyed the unique scenery and atmosphere of the *Black Forest*. It lies along the east bank of the *Rhine* starting at the Swiss frontier and extending north as far as *Karlsruhe*.

Over recent years the forest has become much more accessible. There are good roads and an extended network for walking trails. It is not, by any means, all forest either. There are rolling hills covered in grass and flowers. There are lakes and rivers and for winter sports enthusiasts, ski jumps and trails.

Starting point

An attractive route to the *Black Forest (Schwarzwald)* is via the western bank of the *Rhine* through beautiful French villages and towns with German names − a legacy of the time before World War Two when this area was removed from Germany and became part of France under the Versailles Agreement. Before crossing the river try to find time to look round the stage-set like town of Colmar, then cross into Germany at *Breisach am Rhein* a few miles from *Freiburg*, the capital of the *Black Forest* and gateway to its southern region.

Freiburg

Freiburg has a Cathedral *(Münster)*, started in 1120, regarded as one of the finest medieval cathedrals in Germany with a magnificent steeple 380 feet high. The city has narrow alleys and paved streets with fast-flowing streams called *Bächle* which were originally used to carry away the city's waste. Around the *Münsterplatz* (the Cathedral square) is a pedestrian zone with cafés, restaurants and shops — an area well worth exploring, particularly on a Saturday morning when there is an open-air market.

Up the Schauinsland

You would probably enjoy a trip up the nearest mountain, the *Schauinsland*. You can take a cable car to the summit or drive 4210 feet up a curving mountain road used sometimes for car rallies. To find it, you should leave *Freiburg* by the *Günterstalstrasse* to the village of *Günterstal*. You will eventually have to leave your car to climb the final section on foot to enjoy the fantastic panoramic view on clear days of the *Black Forest,* the *Rhine* plain and the French Vosges.

South of Freiburg

South of *Freiburg* is an area which is sometimes called the German Tuscany as it has a mild climate due to the maritime winds blowing up the *Rhine* valley.

Badenweiler

Built on a hillside overlooking the *Rhine* plain is the small spa town of *Badenweiler*. It has been a spa since the first century AD with ruins of a Roman bath and a *Kurpark* with lush subtropical flora including giant Californian redwoods. But it was the modern spa buildings which we remembered most, luxurious and well designed on several levels overlooking most attractive gardens where there are often open air concerts and events to entertain the visitors who are mostly past the prime of youth and generally very well-heeled!

Hell Valley

If you leave *Freiburg* by the N31 to *Titisee* you will travel through *Hell Valley (Höllental)*, a wild and rocky gorge with an entrance known as *Stag Jump (Hirschsprung)* because a stag is said to have jumped from one side to the other. The busy four-lane road climbs up to *Hinterzarten* before reaching *Titisee*, a summer and winter resort built on the shores of the lake whose name it bears. If you could do with a break from driving you could take the train from *Freiburg* to *Titisee*. It is a spectacular half-hour trip on a track built in 1887 which climbs 2050 feet, a national record for German railways.

Titisee

The resort of *Titisee*, the only settlement on the lake, is a busy place particularly on summer weekends, with lots of souvenir shops selling banners, jugs, T-shirts, walking sticks and cuckoo clocks. On a midweek evening, however, it is quieter and we found it easy to park and were able to stroll around the lake very pleasurably. You can walk right round the lake in about one and a half hours.

Up the Feldberg

Titisee is also a good starting-off point for a trip up the *Feldberg* (4900 feet). Take the road to *Todtnau* — the 317 — which goes through the beautiful *Barental* valley and after about 7 miles you will see the car park for the easiest walk to the top, not too strenuous and lots to see. If it is a warm day you might enjoy a slight detour on the way back to the *Feldsee*, a small lake at the foot of *Feldberg*, enclosed in a ring of wooded hills, very quiet and beautiful.

Schluchsee

Just before the car park for the *Feldberg* walk is a minor road — the 500 — which will take you to the *Schluchsee*, an artificial lake also very popular with summer visitors. On our first visit to this area we stayed with a family in a village called *Brünlisbach* past *Schluchsee* on the road to *Grafenhausen*. This little village had its own *Heimatmuseum* (folk museum) and its own lake called, confusingly, *Schluchtsee*. We spent a very happy holiday here. The lady of the house spoke no English and her husband only a little, picked up while a prisoner of war, but they were unfailingly friendly and helpful, suggesting interesting trips and good places to eat.

Roundabout Schluchsee

We explored the surrounding area visiting interesting small towns such as *St. Blasien* with its magnificently domed and decorated church, *Todtmoos* and *Schönau* from where we drove to the top of the 4,637 foot *Belchen*. *Todtnauberg*, the highest situated resort in the *Black Forest* is well worth a visit with its delightful setting above a cascade of waterfalls. A little further away near *Schaffhausen* on the Swiss border are the spectacular *Rhine Falls*, a foaming mass of water nearly 500 feet wide dropping 21 metres with a thunderous sound. Longer trips included visits to *Konstanz* on *Bodensee* and into Switzerland at *Basel* and *Zurich*.

The "clock country" around Triberg

If you have plenty of time for your return journey you can explore the northern part of the Black Forest by starting on the road north through *Neustadt* to *Furtwangen*. This area around *Furtwangen* is famous for its clockmaking and in the *Uhrenmuseum* you can see clocks of every size and design imaginable. One famous example has a figure of a tailor who, every hour on the hour, is knocked on the head with a shoe by his wife. In *Schonach*, a little further north, you can see the largest cuckoo clock on earth, 23 feet long, 25 feet wide and 21 feet high with a bird which measures 3 feet. You will see a lot of souvenir-type tat but it is worth looking carefully in some of the countless "clock shops" which line the streets of *Furtwangen*, *Schönwald* and *Triberg* if you are in the market for something a little out of the ordinary.

A waterfall and a trainride

Just before you get to *Triberg* you might enjoy a trip to the famous *Gutach* waterfall – the highest in Germany – where the water cascades down 338 feet. Another highly recommended trip is the train ride from *Triberg* (or from *St.*

Georgen a few miles further east) to *Hausach* on the *Schwarzwaldbahn* (the Black Forest railway). This is considered the most spectacular ride on the German railways.

Open-air museum

Just south of *Hausach*, pay a visit to the *Vogtsbauernhof* Museum, an open-air museum containing typical traditional *Black Forest* farmhouses and other buildings, each complete with household utensils and furnishings and farming equipment.

Freudenstadt

Then on to *Freudenstadt*, a modern hill resort which claims to have more hours of sunshine than anywhere else in Germany as well as the biggest marketplace. It is known as "the *Black Forest* crossroads" because three major tourist routes meet here. The *Freundshaftstrasse* (Friendship Road) takes visitors back to the west and the Rhine plain on an extremely scenic route; on the *Schwarzwald-Baderstrasse (Black Forest spa road)* you can go north-east towards *Pforzheim;* while the *Schwarzwald-Hochstrasse* (Black Forest High Road) leads north-west to *Baden-Baden*.

Baden-Baden

You will probably decide to take this road — which runs through a succession of attractive villages — as you cannot leave the *Black Forest* without a visit to the most famous and luxurious spa town of all, *Baden-Baden*. It has a beautiful situation with spa springs, gardens and the *Kurhaus* which includes not only the pump-rooms for the famous spa water but also an enormous and renowned gambling hall which was opened in 1838. In those days, if you were a member of the European aristocracy, a poet or a musician, it was fashionable to spend the summer in *Baden-Baden* where you would hope to find some of Europe's aristocracy — even the English Queen Victoria — in residence.

Present day *Baden-Baden* is for enjoyment and relaxation rather than sight-seeing. There are fashionable hotels and shops, an opera house, art gallery, plentiful sports facilities from tennis to riding as well as the famous *Kurhaus*. In the *Trinkhalle* or pump-room you can drink the medicinal waters or take a mud bath. In addition to these old "cures", *Baden-Baden* now offers "anti-stress" treatments perhaps needed by visitors who lose too much in the casino.

The Black Forest spa road

If, on leaving *Freudenstadt*, you choose the *Pforzheim* road (the *Schwarzwald-Bäderstrasse*) you will come first to *Altensteig*, a small town with gabled houses rising one above the other up to the church and the foot of a castle, and then to the village of *Calw* where there is a medieval bridge which supports a Gothic chapel. Shortly after leaving *Calw* you can take a turning going west — the 296 — to reach a crossroads at *Calmbach*.

A most unusual museum

Turn north at *Calmbach* to *Neuenberg* then west again and you will come across a most unusual museum at the village of *Marxzell*.

When we passed by there some years ago our attention was drawn by some rusty old railway engines by the side of the road. Stopping to investigate, we discovered a very personal museum owned by an old gentleman who is an enthusiast for all kinds of vehicles and anything remotely to do with them. Several sheds are packed — and I mean packed! — with memorabilia of all kinds, hanging from the roof, strung across walls and open spaces, and wedged so tightly together that there is no hope of seeing more than a quarter of the exhibits. In one room he has a collection of pianos, organs and other keyboard instruments which he demonstrates in a lively performance whenever a few visitors are gathered together. Don't miss it if you can arrange your route to be anywhere near!

Heidelberg

From either *Baden-Baden* or *Marxzell* it is a short trip up the motorway to *Heidelberg*, which you might wish to fit into your journey back. *Heidelberg* is one of Germany's most visited tourist attractions famous for its history and its castle, which can be reached on foot up the steep *Burgweg*, by car (there is a car park at the top) or by cable railway. There is the replica of the world-renowned jawbone of *Heidelberg Man* to be seen, and, of course, the university — popularised in the early twentieth century operetta *"The Student Prince"*. *Heidelberg* has a picture-postcard setting on the bank of the beautiful river *Neckar*. It is, however, often packed with tourists which may detract from its appeal.

Heidelberg is, of course, very close to a network of motorways which will take you speedily back to Holland, Belgium, or France and your port of departure.

CHAPTER THIRTEEN: TO EAST BAVARIA

A Bavarian "knees-up"

One memorable evening of our holiday in *East Bavaria* was spent at a *Hüttenabend* (Hut evening) in the foothills just outside *Viechtach*. The local tourist office had sold us tickets saying that a bus would collect us from the market square that evening. Sure enough a smart double decker coach arrived to collect us and the rest of the participants, very few of whom were English, and delivered us to the outskirts of a village in the hills. We were then escorted on a walk of about 2 miles up to the *Kroneberg Hütte* — a walkers' and skiers' refuge and bar — high in the hills overlooking magnificent views. We had a tankard of beer with bread and cheese rolls and were initiated into the procedures of a real Bavarian "knees-up". Music was provided by an accordian and drums, a girl played the zither, the three waitresses sang and another young lady provided apparently uproarious and probably somewhat risqué monologues of which we could, unfortunately, understand virtually nothing. At the end of a great evening's entertainment which included a good deal of foot stamping, armlinking and swaying, a short announcement was all it took to persuade the entire company to move outside to surround an enormous bonfire and sing romantic songs before setting out on the walk back to the coach, with our guides carrying lanterns to light our way. Don't turn down the chance of a *Hüttenabend* if you hear of one on your travels.

The Bavarian Forest

East Bavaria is situated on the far side of West Germany and borders Czechoslovakia on its eastern side and Austria to the south. The most easterly part right against the border is known as the *Bavarian Forest*. The Green Michelin Guide describes it as an area which "attracts visitors with simple tastes who enjoy solitude". The small, pretty towns and villages are summer resorts providing swimming, fishing and walking as well as winter resorts for cheap and simple skiing holidays. The air is clean and unpolluted and is often advertised as a *Luftkur* (air cure) by towns who lack "spa" type medicinal springs. Accommodation in this area is probably still less expensive than anywhere else in Germany.

We visited *East Bavaria* to stay in a small town called *Viechtach* known, we were told, as "the green heart of Bavaria". The package holiday from the Olau brochure gave a choice of accommodation in hotels, guesthouses, private houses, apartments or camping holidays. It is quite a long journey − almost over to the Czechoslovakian border − so it is best to work out an interesting route and make the journey part of the holiday by visiting lots of places on the way.

The Lahn Valley

Starting from *Koblenz*, you could head up the *Lahn* Valley which separates the *Westerwald* from the *Taunus* areas. It is on the edge of a volcanic region and is rich in mineral springs, ruined castles and small towns. The first town is a small spa, *Bad Ems*, famous because the *Kaiser* chose it for his annual "cure". It is an attractive place laid out on both sides of the *Lahn* which from here on becomes even more picturesque.

You then pass through a small fortified village called *Dausenau* before reaching *Nassau*, another attractive health resort where there is a Nature Park. The road then leaves the river for a while before rejoining it at *Limburg* where the cathedral with its setting on a spur of rock dominates the attractive town centre. Then on to the motorway near

Wiesbaden, by-passing *Frankurt*, on the way to *Aschaffenburg*.

Aschaffenburg

Now you will have arrived in *Bavaria* although you are still only 25 miles south east of *Frankfurt*. *Aschaffenburg* is an important cultural and trade centre with some outstanding buildings and beautiful parks. It is also the gateway to *Spessart*, a region of forested hills, small towns and villages and a maze of footpaths which make the region ideal for hikers.

Nuremberg

From *Aschaffenburg*, the A3 motorway will take you to *Nuremberg*, the second largest city in *Bavaria* and an important industrial, commercial and cultural centre described in Chapter Eighteen.

East Bavaria

When you arrive in *East Bavaria*, spend an hour or two looking round *Cham*, a pretty town on the *Regen* river. A few miles further on is *Viechtach* where we stayed in the *Gasthof Waldemülhe* which was most attractive, a typically Alpine chalet-type building set on a wooded hillside overlooking the village with every balcony and windowsill decked with brightly coloured geraniums. Our room was well-furnished, with a good-sized private bathroom, television, and a balcony overlooking the hills and valleys surrounding the area.

No-one at the *Gasthof* spoke English but all were friendly and helpful and with our phrase book and our "First Year German" we managed to get along famously. One evening we went down to the bar/dining room for a drink and found another English couple sitting with the owner. He spoke no English and they spoke no German but they were cementing international relations over several large glasses of beer and small glasses of Schnapps. They were glad to have us join them – mainly to act as interpreters, I think – and it is amazing how long you can "chat" even when comprehension is limited!

Viechtach

Viechtach, like the other small towns and villages in the area, is a small summer and winter resort where discerning holiday makers can enjoy good skiing in winter and plenty of walking, exploring, fishing and swimming — in an excellent heated outdoor pool — in summer.

The area round Viechtach

Enjoyable days can be spent just wandering round the beautiful countryside, with no traffic jams, no noise and bustle, enjoying the peace of the *Bavarian Forest* region. Quite close at hand, near the village of *Weissenregen*, there is a tiny whitewashed chapel very simple looking from the outside but inside breathtakingly baroque, everything painted in gleaming shades of pink and blue and gold. You could climb (or ride in a chair-lift) to the top of the *Grosser Arber*, at 4780 feet the highest mountain in *East Bavaria* with its two lakes, the *Grosser* and *Kliener Arbersee*. Or visit the nearby glass-making town of *Zwiesel* and the prosperous spa-town *Bodenmais*. Go to *Lohberg*, the highest village in the forest, surrounded by woodland with a game enclosure, a keep-fit trail with exercise points and lots of marked walks along the banks of the *Kleiner Arbersee*. Explore the National Park with its thirty-six marked paths and nature trails or drive alongside the Czechoslovakian border — recently an area of green no-mans-land, a few signs and, among the trees, a glimpse of a watch-tower. Even these have probably disappeared now and it may well be possible to drive across the border at the small town of *Bayerisch Eisenstein* or to take a day trip by coach to *Prague*. If you wish to do this enquire at the local tourist office. It used to be necessary to give at least a week's notice and complete an application form with a photograph but it is likely that these formalities have now been relaxed.

The Drachenstich Festival in Fürth im Wald

Should your holiday include the second Sunday in August, you will not want to miss the *Drachenstich*, the dragon sticking festival, at *Fürth im Wald*. This has grown from a country pageant to a major production which is performed in the main street with seating for over two thousand people. The fantastic dragon — which can be seen on non-Festival days in the *Schlossplatz* for a small fee — is 50 feet long, 13 feet wide and 10 feet tall with wings which flap and jaws which open and shut to show its wicked teeth! If you miss the *Drachenstich, Fürth* is still worth a visit as it is an attractive town with a carillon of bells which plays at 11am.

Steam train rides

On a Sunday morning you could take a ride in a steam train on the Regen Valley Railway between *Kötzting* and *Lam* or from *Viechtach* to the neighbouring village of *Blaibach*. You may well be accompanied by a large group of cheery Bavarians with an oom-pah band and many crates of beer!

Regensburg

One day might be spent visiting *Regensburg* and *Kelheim*. *Regensburg* itself is an interesting and historic town. It is at the northernmost navigable point of the Danube and boats can travel from here right downstream to the Black Sea. It did not suffer a great deal during World War II and its Roman and medieval treasures and buildings are as interesting as its more modern city centre and lively port area. While you are wandering, try to find time to visit the *Steinerne Brücke* — a stone bridge across the *Danube* which is reputed to be the oldest bridge in Germany and which provides an excellent view of the stately mansions along the river side and the spires of the *Dom* (Cathedral). The *Dom*, apart from its collection of Gothic sculptures, fourteenth century stained glass and other ecclesiastical treasures is also famous for its boys choir, the *Regensburger Domspatzen*. There are good restaurants offering local delicacies, such as *Wels*, a Danube fish, or *Tafelspitz*, boiled beef, or you could visit the

Historische Wurstküche, the old sausage kitchen, built 800 years ago to provide food for the workmen building the *Steinerne Brücke* and now feeding equally hungry tourists with delicious *Regensburg* sausages and potato soup. The *Ratskeller* (the Town Hall cellar restaurant) will provide a cheap snack or a good set lunch.

Excursion to Walhalla

There are two particularly notable excursions from *Regensburg*. The first is to *Walhalla*, the Hall of Fame, designed by the Bavarian King Ludwig I and built in 1830−1842 in the style of the Greek Parthenon. From the terrace in front of the monument, seven miles east of the city, there is a marvellous view of the *Danube* valley − on a clear day you can even see the Alps.

To Kelheim

The second trip to be made from *Regensburg* is to *Kelheim* for a beautiful walk or boat ride up the *Danube* to the monastery (*Kloster*) at *Weltenburg*. The scenery is spectacular as the river narrows and forces its way through limestone cliffs which tower about 400 feet above the river. On the right bank there is a footpath providing a pleasant clearly-marked forest walk which takes about one hour, or you can take the motor boat which plies frequently up and down starting from the jetty in *Kelheim*.

Passau

Another interesting trip is to *Passau* set on a narrow point of land where the rivers *Inn*, *Ilz* and *Danube* come together. The town is dominated by the fifteenth century cathedral which has an octagonal dome as well as two towers. Inside, it boasts the largest church organ in the world with 17,300 pipes and 231 stops. Most visitors to *Passau* converge on the *Dom* just before noon each day when there is a free organ recital. If you arrive in the town at about 11.30am you may find it virtually impossible to park. Do try to find a place to stop as this beautiful and unusual city warrants exploration

on foot. With its steep, narrow and cobbled one-way streets, the houses joined together by archways and its busy water-front, it is quite unsuited to the age of the motor car.

Passau is right on the Austrian border and you can drive into that country with little bother if you wish to do so. The countryside immediately over the border is, however, not particularly "Austrian" as it is still the *Danube* valley and some miles away from the Alps and lakes.

Cruises down the Danube

Passau is also a starting point for boat trips to *Regensburg* or cruises down the *Danube* as far as *Vienna* or the Black Sea.

Beer Festival at Straubing

Our visit during August happened to coincide with the annual *Gäubodenfest* in nearby *Straubing*. With at least seven beer tents, a huge amusement park and 900,000 visitors every year, it provides an opportunity to experience the *Oktoberfest* atmosphere. A slight snag was that we found ourselves stuck in an horrendous traffic jam on the outskirts of the town. Once at the parking fields, however, everything was organised with typical German efficiency and Bavarian *Gemütlichkeit*. It is a cross between the Bath and West Show, the Ideal Home exhibition and a funfair with the addition of the enormous beer tents where great quantities of ale are sold in vast one litre tankards called *Mass*. The dirndl-skirted waitresses somehow manage to carry up to ten of these heavy, enormous glasses at one time and keep the beer flowing freely!

Ferry across the Danube

We decided to try a more circuitous route back to *Viechtach* to avoid the traffic jams again and found ourselves unexpectedly on the wrong side of the *Danube* near the village of *Stephansposching*. We had to cross to the companion village of *Mariasposching* on the opposite bank by a small car ferry which held just six cars and was propelled by an uncertain engine and a man with a large pole. (I am sure there must be a story behind the names and positions of these two villages but I have not been able to discover it yet!)

Starting back

All too soon your time in *East Bavaria* will come to an end and you must set out on the long journey back to England. If you have stayed too long it will probably mean a fast trip back on the *Autobahn* via *Nuremberg, Frankfurt* and *Cologne* but if you have time there is much to see on the way back. The most obvious first stop would be the Bavarian capital of *Munich*, described in Chapter Eighteen.

Home via the Romantic Road

An attractive route home from *Munich* is to carry on to *Augsberg* where you can join the *Romantic Road* which you can follow through *Donauwörth, Harburg, Nördlingen,* and *Dinkelsbühl* — and which you will find described in detail in Chapter Fourteen.

Schwäbisch Hall

If you leave the *Romantic Road* after *Dinkelsbühl*, your next stop could be *Schwäbisch Hall*, the most picturesque town in the *Swabian Forest* region and worth a visit to see its half-timbered houses set in terraces built into the hillside, two wooden bridges spanning the river and a most rococo *Rathaus*. Then across to *Heidelberg* and up to *Mainz* to join the *Rhine Valley* route home — see Chapter Eleven.

CHAPTER FOURTEEN:
FOLLOWING THE ROMANTIC ROAD

This route from *Würzburg* in the North to *Füssen* in the South was the first and is one of the longest of Germany's many named tourist routes — about 200 miles. On your journey you will have the opportunity to admire most of the varied forms of European architecture — from Romanesque, Gothic, Renaissance, Baroque, and Rococo to Neo-classicism. It will take you through at least eight different types of landscape each outdoing the other with a variety of attractions and traditions.

Würzburg

Würzburg, the official northern starting point has long been regarded as one of the great cities of Europe often sadly neglected by tourists. Situated about 1½ hours journey from *Frankfurt*, it is on the banks of the river Main and boasts two superb buildings: the *Residenz* and the *Marienberg* Castle. The *Residenz* was built between 1720 and 1780 and has a magnificent Emperor's hall. This is decorated with a fine ceiling fresco by Tiepolo and is lit by hundreds of candles during the annual Mozart festival which takes place in June. The building was damaged by bombing in the last days of World War Two and has been wonderfully restored. The *Marienberg* which is on top of a hill on the other side of the river, was founded in 1201 and has had many additions and alterations since then.

Across the street from the *Residenz* are the Bavarian State Wine Cellars where visitors are welcomed to the wine tastings which take place almost every day. Leave time for a wander down through the town to the *Alte Mainbrücke* (the old bridge over the river Main) to see the view and the baroque figures carved into the bridge itself. Wine lovers might also like to follow the *Stein* Wine trail on the northern edge of the town. This is an educational path just under three miles long through one of the best known German vineyard areas. October, when the grapes are picked, is the best time for a visit to the vineyards of *Franconia*. Wine festivals are held each weekend in villages in the area while in *Würzburg* itself the Wine Producers' Festival lasts for about ten days from the end of September.

The Romantic Road leaves *Würzburg* as *Bundesstrasse No.8* and winds through the suburb of *Höchberg* where you must watch for the sign *Romantischestrasse* (Romantic Road) and join the B27 towards *Tauberbischofsheim*.

Tauberbischofsheim

The road will take you down the pretty *Tauber* valley through woods and hilly farmland to *Tauberbischofsheim*, a compact old medieval town surrounded by a ring road with several free car parks which it is wise to use as it is quite a hassle trying to park in the narrow streets of the old town. The lower part was devastated by floods in 1985 and as you wander through the town you may notice small plaques which mark the level to which the water rose at that time.

Bad Mergentheim

On leaving *Tauberbischofsheim* continue down the *Tauber* valley on the B29 through villages with baroque churches and half-timbered buildings towards *Bad Mergentheim*. From the sixteenth to the eighteenth century, this was the headquarters of the Teutonic Order of Knights and their castle is still the great sight of the city. In 1809 the order was dissolved by Napoleon and the citizens of *Mergentheim* feared their days of affluence were numbered. Very fortuitously, just a few years later, a shepherd tending his sheep on the hillside on the north bank of the river discovered mineral water springs.

Mergentheim, soon to be renamed *Bad Mergentheim*, (*Bad* in German meaning "bath") came back to new life as a spa town boasting four healing springs which are supposed to help cure diseases of the liver, gall-bladder, kidneys and other organs.

There are good facilities for tourists including a leisure centre called *Solymar* which has a pool with artificial waves as well as a mineral spring pool and a heated open-air swimming pool with a bar and restaurant for spectators.

It is a prosperous and busy market town with good shops as well as the attraction of the ancient buildings which are open to the public. You can enjoy *Kaffee und Kuchen* (coffee and cakes) in the *Café in der Schlossgarten* (The cafe in the castle garden), a courtyard garden hidden away inside the castle which is now used as municipal offices and museum.

Weikersheim

On leaving *Bad Mergentheim* follow the B19 in the direction back to *Würzburg* but turn south again shortly on a road signposted *"Rothenburg"* through a broad valley lined with vineyards to *Weikersheim*, a small town with a castle. The eighteenth century marketplace is semicircular on one side providing a vista of the palace which is open to the public. It is magnificently furnished with tapestries, portraits and porcelain and has cellars containing great casks of wine. The *Schlosspark*, castle park, is also open to the public and has fine baroque gardens with colourful flower beds, an orangery and many amusing statues.

Röttingen

Keep travelling east and six km later you will arrive at the village of *Röttingen* which has a wine and theatre festival in July and August which attracts visitors from a wide area. *Röttingen* has a baroque *Rathaus*, an attractive *Marktplatz* and an old town wall with seven towers providing an unspoiled medieval scene.

Creglingen

The valley narrows above the attractive town of *Bieberehren* where the vineyards end and the slopes are covered with woodland and orchards which are particularly attractive in springtime. The small town of *Creglingen* is just off the main road and has ample free parking for the many visitors who come to visit the Church of the Crucifix to see the famous wooden altar piece carved in the early sixteenth century by *Tilman Riemenschneider*, a master carver from *Würzburg*. Another of his famous pieces can be seen in the village of *Detwang* just before reaching *Rothenburg*.

Rothenburg ob der Tauber

This is the most famous stop on the *Romantic Road*. The town, surrounded by its ramparts and towers, has remained virtually as it was in medieval times with a few Renaissance additions. As in York, in England, it is possible to walk round the town on its ramparts. It is perhaps a good idea to do this first as it provides marvellous panoramic views at almost every turn. If you stop off at the gate called *Koboldzellertor* and look down to the river *Tauber* you will be able to see the old *Dopperbrücke*, a remarkable twelfth century double-decker stone bridge. There is plenty to see in *Rothenburg*; yet another Riemenschneider altarpiece; *der Meistertrunk* clock which plays every day at 11, 12, 1 and 2 o'clock in memory of a drinking feat which saved the city from destruction in 1631; numerous fountains lined with scarlet geraniums; excellent restaurants and cafés; the medieval and Renaissance *Rathaus*. Really the best thing to do in *Rothenburg* is to wander and absorb the atmosphere. It is a very busy place with hundreds of coachloads of visitors during most days so you might arrange to stay overnight either in the town or, more economically, in one of the surrounding villages so that you can wander round in the quiet of the early morning and evening hours when the coaches have departed and the town returns to the peace which seems much more appropriate.

Schillingfürst Castle

As you leave *Rothenburg*, taking the B25 south towards *Feuchtwangen*, you will no doubt glance back occasionally to take a last look at the ramparts and towers but look ahead also to catch a glimpse of the baroque castle of *Schillingfürst*. It is set among the wooded *Frankenhöhe* (Franconian Heights) at a point which is the watershed between the *Tauber* and the *Wörnitz* rivers. It can, therefore, be said that water from the castle may go either via the *Tauber* and *Rhine* to the North Sea, or to the Black Sea with the *Wörnitz* and the *Danube*. The castle, finished in 1750, was at one time the home of Franz Liszt and there is a statue of the great composer in the park.

Feuchtwangen

Still on the B25, about 17 kilometres after leaving *Rothenburg*, you will reach *Feuchtwangen*, a small township with a tranquil and sedate atmosphere. It is somewhat over-shadowed by the proximity of *Rothenburg* except in July and August when the Romanesque cloisters are the setting for open air theatre performances and craft workshops.

Dinkelsbühl

A short journey of 13 kilometres brings you to my favourite place on the Romantic Road, *Dinkelsbühl*. Fodor describes *Dinkelsbühl* as "a medieval town which has drifted off to sleep" and I find it hard to improve on that description. The town wall with its twenty towers is lined with green meadows, ponds, vegetable gardens, orchards and a moat. The medieval quality is maintained as houses have to be restored or rebuilt according to the traditional half-timbering method and the signs over shops and restaurants are master-pieces of wrought-iron sculpture sometimes extravagantly gilded. Every evening a night watchman goes on his rounds through the streets singing his message that "all is well." A little gem of a place with lots to see and a choice of good places to eat and stay. Don't miss *Dinkelsbühl*.

Nördlingen

Next comes *Nördlingen*, a bigger and busier version of *Dinkelsbühl*. It has a unique situation at the centre of a 16 mile-wide shallow crater which was studied by the NASA astronauts and is now believed to have been caused when an enormous meteorite struck the earth fifteen million years ago. In the thirteenth century, *Nördlingen* became a free Imperial City and hub of trade for most of southern Germany, able to finance the town walls and battlements which are still an outstanding attraction for visitors. The roofed parapet walk along the walls is over two miles long and still intact. It provides a wonderful way to stroll round the town and get a bird's eye view of its half-timbered houses and narrow streets.

Harburg

About ten miles further — still going south-east on the B25 — you reach the banks of the river *Wörnitz* and the little town of *Harburg* overlooked by its mighty thirteenth century castle which has been much enlarged and now houses a museum of art treasures including illuminated manuscripts and engravings.

Donauwörth

Soon the *Wörnitz* joins the *Danube* at *Donauwörth*, another medieval town with old town walls and gates and other historical monuments, many of which needed to be rebuilt after the bombing raids of World War Two. One which was left intact was the *Riedertor*, a gate close to the town hall, from which a bridge leads to the original fishermen's quarter on *Wörnitz* Island.

Augsburg

The next part of the Road — the B2 — is of less interest until in 43 km you drive through the Red Gate into the greatest metropolis on the Romantic Road, *Augsburg*. Its wide and imposing main street, *Maximilianstrasse*, with its beautiful Renaissance fountains and its gabled houses, leads to the

Rathaus (town hall) designed by one *Elias Holl*, who was the municipal architect for other sixteenth-century buildings in *Augsburg*. One of the towers is still used as a watch-tower and a yellow flag is flown when it is clear enough to see the Alps from its top. Other sights in the neighbourhood are the Augustus fountain and the cathedral, where there are Mozart concerts in the summer. Mozart's father was born quite close by and the house is now a museum. Slightly further away is the *Fuggerai*, the world's first low-price housing project built in 1514 to salve the conscience of the rich *Jacob Fugger* after he had built his luxurious *Fuggerhaus* in *Maximilianstrasse*. The annual rent for a small flat was one old Rhenish florin (now about 1.72*DM*) and it is still the same today for those lucky enough to live here. It is a peaceful and secluded backwater of eight streets with about 60 gabled houses and pretty gardens inside four gateways which are closed each night to preserve the peace of the neighbourhood and allow the inhabitants time to remember the founder in their prayers.

The Lech Valley

Leaving *Augsburg*, on the B17 south following the valley of the river *Lech*, you come to *Klosterlechfeld*, where there is another Renaissance church designed by Elias Holl, and then to *Landsberg* built to guard the frontier between *Bavaria* and *Swabia* and the only bridge across the *Lech* between *Augsburg* and *Schöngau*. The original town walls and towers are still there as is the rococo town hall (which is now also the information office). Also in *Landsberg* but not open to the public, is the *Landsberg* fortress where Hitler wrote *Mein Kampf* during 1923–24 while he was imprisoned after the failure of the *Munich Putsch*.

Approaching the Alps

Continuing on the B17, the *Romantic Road* takes a picturesque route following the *Lech* valley with its dairy cattle country and baroque and rococo churches. On a clear day, the outline of the Alps becomes discernable on the southern skyline.

Schongau

When you reach *Hohenfurch* you are into the foothills and, five kilometres further on, *Schongau* calls itself "the town in front of the mountains". This was once an important stop on the medieval trade route and still has old city walls, towers and several historical buildings. Visitors can enjoy swimming in the heated pools or from the beaches on the *Schongauer See*, an eight km long lake where it is also possible to sail, canoe or wind-surf. A short detour allows a trip to *Hohenpeissenberg*, 3260 feet up, and a fantastic view of some eleven lakes as well as the range of mountains including the *Bavarian Alps*.

Allgäu

Back on the B17, you will reach *Steingaden*, another holiday resort catering for winter and summer visitors, before arriving at the area known as *Allgäu*, with the lakes of *Bannwaldsee* and *Forggensee* and, for many the climax of the *Romantic Road*, the famous castles of *Hohenschwangau* and *Neuschwanstein* with their turrets and pinnacles amidst the spectacular backdrop of mountains. They are described in more detail in Chapter Sixteen.

Füssen

A few miles further on and 350 kilometres since we started at *Würzburg*, we come to the last stop on the *Romantischestrasse* at *Füssen*, an old mountain town which originally guarded a pass through the Alps giving it perfect scenic surroundings. Good facilities here for either a winter skiing holiday or summer water-sports or walking amidst mountains, lakes and streams based on this small picturesque town which marks the end of our journey down Germany's most famous *Romantic Road*.

CHAPTER FIFTEEN:
TO THE NORTH SEA AND BALTIC COASTS

The North Sea coast of Germany bears little resemblance to the North Sea coast of Britain. The coastline from Den Helder, just north of Amsterdam, to Esbjerg in Southern Denmark is lined with off-shore islands, often little more than sandbanks, which have been defended from the encroaching sea for centuries. On the mainland there is wide, open countryside edged with miles of sandy beaches and rolling dunes. A popular area for peaceful, sunny seaside holidays attracting visitors from Germany and from further afield.

If you have driven round the coast of northern Holland you will already have seen and possibly visited the West Frisian islands. You will have grown accustomed to the flat landscape dotted with areas of water and you will notice little difference when you first cross into Germany shortly after leaving Groningen.

Leer

The first German town you will reach after crossing the river *Ems*, is *Leer*. It is a picturesque old market town which claims to have the largest cattle market in north-western Germany. The centre of the town has been pedestrianised and is well worth a stroll. Keep an eye open in these small towns for the modern statues which seem to have become a feature of German shopping precincts. The one in *Leer* is of a group of children — two girls trying to hold back a small boy who is leaning precariously over the edge of a fountain.

From Emden — a visit to Borkum

If you take the B70 northwards from *Leer* you will be
heading for *Emden*, once the hiding place of pirates and now
the largest car-shipping port in Europe. It is also the starting
point for a 2½ hour trip to *Borkum*, the largest and the most
westerly of the *Frisian Islands*. On most of the islands, cars
are not permitted but limited access is allowed on *Borkum*,
where there is also a small airfield which offers the opportunity of inter-island flights. There are spa facilities, a casino
and plenty of accommodation but the real thing to do on
Borkum, as on the other islands, is to enjoy a relaxing holiday
on the bathing beaches on the seaward side and the nature
reserves on the tidal southern mudflats where you can enjoy
birdwatching, horse riding or cycling along the paths among
the dunes. The air is said to be highly beneficial to those suffering from catarrh or hay fever.

Aurich and the East Frisian Islands

Further along the coast, the other *East Frisian Islands* are
closer to the coast with a correspondingly shorter boat ride.
Take the B70 from *Emden* to *Aurich*, a pleasant modern small
town with good supermarkets and an excellent information
office. Our visit to *Aurich* was memorable because of a most
unusual and very destructive storm which blew up suddenly
at the end of a perfect day and departed again just as suddenly
an hour or two later, leaving behind a trail of uprooted and
decapitated trees along a stretch of road perhaps three miles
long. The German emergency services proved themselves
extremely capable. While the storm was still raging teams of
workmen were out, removing fallen trees and generally
tidying up and within an hour or two the roads were open
again and life back to normal.

The Tourist Office in *Aurich* will advise you on the starting
points for boat trips to the various islands. You will notice
from your *Kümmerly + Frey* map of *Niedersachsen (Lower
Saxony)* that each one leaves from a different small port along
the nearby coast. The services in summer are quite frequent
and run exactly to timetable but do check on the times for

the day you wish to visit as at low tide the boats have to make their way to the islands through deep water channels marked by lines of saplings.

Nordeney

The trip to *Nordeney* starts at the small port of *Norddeich*. There is also a service to *Juist* (on which the main means of transport is horse-drawn coaches) and to *Baltrum*, the smallest of the islands.

Nordeney is the oldest North Sea resort in Germany having welcomed visitors since 1797. Still an elegant spa and resort with some good hotels, it has an international reputation and you may well see yachts lying offshore flying the flags of many different nations. It has a heated sea-water swimming pool with artificial waves as well as excellent beaches, some of which are reserved for nudists. Swimming or even sun-bathing in the nude seems a reasonable occupation but I must admit seeing people with no clothes queueing for the toilets or ice creams seems rather more incongruous. I was particularly amused by one old gentleman wearing nothing but his cap!

After wandering round the main town area, a good way to see the rest of the island is to hire a bicycle and ride on the excellent paths among the sand dunes which stretch round most of the coastline.

Langeoog

Langeoog is smaller but higher, having large dunes which rise to 30 feet! When you disembark you can avoid the long walk down the straight road into town by taking a ride on a small train, with every coach a different brightly painted colour, which delivers you to the town of *Langeoog* on the seaward side of the island. There is no other form of motor-ised transport so it's back to bicycles to get to see its small air field, excellent bathing beaches, bird sanctuaries and yacht harbour.

Other Islands

Spiekeroog is a haven for nature lovers as half the island is designated as a nature reserve. It has a bus service as well as horse-drawn coaches and can be visited from *Neuharlingersiel*.

Wangerooge is mainly known as a health resort and can be reached by a boat from *Harlesiel*.

Helgoland

From most of these little ports you can, in the summer season, also take a longer boat ride to *Helgoland* (we call it Heligoland, a name once well-known in our shipping forecasts). The island is better known to German holiday makers for its red limestone cliffs which provide exciting walks, good bathing from the sheltered sandy beaches or the sea-water indoor/outdoor pools, and its tax-free spirits and tobacco. At the end of World War II everything in *Helgoland* was blown up by the Allies to destroy the wartime submarine base. Most of the pastel-coloured buildings on the island are, therefore, new and there is a modern elevator connecting the lower and upper parts of the town. The island also has a daily boat service from *Cuxhaven* and a summer service from *Hamburg*.

Crossing the Weser and the Elbe

The North Frisian Islands are further round the coast and you will have to continue your journey by crossing the rivers *Weser* and *Elbe*. Try to spare time for a visit to *Bremen* on the way.

Bremen

The main road crossing will take you into the city of *Bremen*. One of the few cities in Germany with a population of over half a million, it is a port, a commercial town with important exchanges particularly in coffee and cotton, as well as a city of culture and history. Its old streets have been skilfully restored after suffering much damage in the war and the *Rathaus* and the market place are well worth seeing.

Ferry crossings

A new motorway route across the *Weser* and the *Elbe* north of *Hamburg* is planned for the future. In the meantime, if you do not want to go inland to *Bremen* it is possible to cross both rivers by car ferries which provide a break for the driver as well as a good view of the surrounding countryside. Route B435 from *Aurich* leads directly to the ferry across the *Weser* south of *Bremerhaven* and continues as the B495 to take you to the longer ferry crossing across the *Elbe* near *Glückstadt*. This will give an opportunity of visiting the great North German city, *Hamburg*.

Hamburg

You will notice as you drive along in this area that on most of the cars the number plate begins with the letters HH. This denotes that they are registered in "the Free and Hanseatic city of Hamburg". It is Germany's second city and one of Europe's biggest ports, situated on the river *Elbe* more than 60 miles from the open sea. An interesting and exciting city, *Hamburg*, which is described in Chapter Eighteen, is well worth a visit.

St. Peter Ording

Driving north on the motorway from *Hamburg*, you will reach *St. Peter Ording*, an unusual seaside resort on the *Eiderstedt* peninsula. Known as a climatic health resort thanks to its air, said to be rich in iodine, its salt-water and sulphur "cures" and mud-baths, *St. Peter*, like the other small resorts along this coast, has miles of sand, some of which is covered at high tide with shallow, relatively warm, water. Cars park on the sand and about a quarter of a mile out to sea, there are buildings on stilts which provide cafes, toilets and the other essentials which you would normally find on the promenade of a seaside town. Further out towards the edge of the water are the wicker chairs called *"Korbs"* which seem to be a speciality of this northern coast. These are large reclining chairs for two people in which you can sit, sleep,

change or do whatever you wish once you have hired one for the day or week.

When the tide is about to come in a loud speaker announcement will get the car drivers reluctantly moving their vehicles closer towards the shore but the chair sitters will often remain unmoving knowing well that the shallow waters, if they reach them at all, will only lap round the low sand banks which they have built around themselves.

The North Frisian Islands

Further north up the coast are similar resorts. From *Husum* you can visit the *Hallogen* islands, tiny patches of marsh in the middle of the mud flats, and the larger islands of *Nordstrand* and *Pellworm* which were once a continuous strip of land but which were separated by floods in the 14th century. From *Husum* or from *Schüttsiel* or *Dagebüll* a little further north, you can take a boat trip to the three bigger *North Frisian Islands*. *Amrum*, the furthest away, has a nine mile long white beach sheltered by high sand-dunes, and many old Frisian houses. *Fohr*, the greenest of the three, has the mildest climate with roses blooming well into winter, and the well-known resort of *Wyk* as its capital. The third island, *Sylt*, the northernmost point of Germany, is known as the "St. Tropez of the north" as in summer thousands of well-to-do people spend their holidays on the excellent beaches of the island. There is also a railway connection across a causeway to *Westerland*, the capital of *Sylt*, popular with families and gamblers!

Across the border to Denmark?

Back on the mainland you will find yourself almost in Denmark and you may decide to cross the border and continue north to *Billand* to visit the famous Legoland or take the coast road to *Esbjerg* from where it is possible to get a ferry back to England.

Flensburg

For those who wish to remain in Germany the next stop is

likely to be *Flensburg*, the most northerly town on the German mainland, founded 700 years ago and for many years an important trading centre. Today it is known as the gateway to Scandinavia and, to most Germans, as the home of the *Kraftfahrzeugbundsamt*, the German equivalent of our Motor Licensing Bureau at Swansea, where all German cars and traffic offences are registered. *Flensburg* has an understandably Danish feel and offers a boat trip around the bay to visit the small neighbouring Danish ports. Close by is beautiful *Glücksburg* Castle situated in the middle of a lovely lake and green forest and open to the public.

The Baltic Coast

From *Flensburg* you can start your return journey down the eastern side of *Schleswig Holstein* and see a little of the Baltic coast. The B199 will take you fairly close to the coast so that you can make the occasional detour to "see the sea", perhaps to the small fishing port of *Massholm* famous for its seafood restaurants whose speciality is smoked eel, or to the white sand beaches where you can hunt for beautiful pebbles and fossils.

Schleswig

From *Kappeln* take the B201 inland to *Schleswig*, the oldest town in the area, dating from Viking times. The ancient cathedral has a famous carved wooden altar. Other sights worth seeing are *Gottdorf*, an imposing castle which houses two important museums, and the Nydam ship, a fourth century Viking boat unearthed from nearby marshes complete with mummified bodies and pieces of their clothes, shoes and weapons.

Kiel

The coast road, now the B76, will take you through *Eckenforde*, a fishing port, on to *Kiel*, the capital and largest industrial city of *Schleswig Holstein*. Its importance grew with the building of the Kiel canal, the *Nord Ostsee Kanal*, connecting the North Sea to the Baltic, and its naval base, both of which were constantly bombed during the last war. Kiel has been rebuilt and is famous for Kiel Week in early summer when yachtsmen and boating enthusiasts from all over the world compete in the regatta competitions. On the coast east of *Kiel* are excellent bathing beaches including *Schönberger Strand* and *Strandbad Californien*.

The Lake District

Inland from *Kiel* is the "lake district", innumerable lakes surrounded by beech and oak forests. Very popular with tourists, it is situated around and between the small towns of *Eutin, Malente-Gremsmühlen* and *Plön*. *Eutin* is a small lakeside town which has a castle with an English-style garden and a park where, in the summer time, music from operas, particularly those by Weber who lived here, are performed in the open air. *Malente-Gremsmühlen* is a spa town between two lakes and a starting point for "five lakes" boat trips while *Plön* is a tourist centre with the largest lake and a Renaissance castle. The area is known as "the Switzerland of Holstein" and has a Swiss feel about it — except that there is not a mountain to be seen!. You could have a very pleasant lakeside holiday exploring this region but if you want to continue your tour of German beaches just travel east from *Kiel* back to the Baltic coast.

Quiet holiday resorts on the Baltic Coast

At *Oldenburg* turn north on the B207 and you can travel over the *Fehmarnsund Brücke* to *Fehmarn* Island and finally to *Püttgarden* where you can take the ferry to Denmark and the motorway network leading to Scandinavia.

Turning south from *Oldenburg* you can take the motorway A1 (E4) to the old town of *Neustadt* or travel still further east on minor roads to find some peaceful holiday resorts on the warmer, sheltered Baltic coast. Look out for *Grömitz, Kellenhausen* and *Dahme*. Further south from *Neustadt* you will find *Scharbeutz, Haffkrug* and *Sierksdorf*.

123

Timmendorfer Strand and Travemünde

You will soon arrive at the more cosmopolitan resorts popular with the people of *Lübeck* and visitors from Scandinavia. First, *Timmendorfer Strand* with its fine white sand beach and beautiful woodland and then *Travemünde*, the beach resort of *Lübeck* and terminal for ferries to *Helsinki, Stockholm* and *Copenhagen*.

Travemünde has a famous and well patronised casino, plenty of hotels, restaurants and nightlife, an enormous enclosed all-year-round swimming pool, and a view of East Germany which is just across a short stretch of water.

Lübeck

Before leaving the area try to find time to visit *Lübeck*. There is plenty to see in this attractive old town with its "brick Gothic" architecture, dating from the twelfth century and its situation on a river island in the *Trave*, the river which reaches the sea at *Travemünde*. The "old town" has a massive fifteenth century gateway, topped by twin turrets. In spite of the ravages of several wars culminating in the bombing suffered in World War II, it is clear that this was a wealthy town with its beautiful churches, gabled houses and its spectacular *Rathaus*. In the cellar of the *Rathaus,* by the way, you can enjoy a cheap lunchtime snack — perhaps a bowl of soup with a local sausage — in most unusual surroundings. Wander round the city, look up the narrow passageways between the buildings lining the streets to see the flowered courtyards, taste the famous *Lübecker* marzipan in the *Niederegger* shop where it is reputed to have originated in 1806. I doubt if you will hear any English voices; *Lübeck* seems to be almost unknown to visitors from this country. And yet it is only 40 miles from *Hamburg* and, if your holiday time is up, it will not take long for you to be back there for your ferry or to start your journey back across Germany and Holland.

CHAPTER SIXTEEN:
ALONG THE ALPINE ROAD

The Alpine Road passes through beautiful countryside by the sides of lakes and around spectacular snow-capped mountains. No other route in Germany can beat this for scenery. There is so much to see on the way that, unless you have a very long holiday, you might need more than one trip to cover the whole route properly. You may well be tempted to linger somewhere which you find particularly attractive and there are many places along the way where you could spend a most enjoyable holiday. Bear in mind that you will already have had quite a long journey to arrive at the starting point on *Lake Constance*.

Although this chapter is headed 'Along the Alpine Road', the journey suggested includes one or two detours and extensions to cover some very interesting places which would otherwise be missed. For example, the official route starts at *Lindau*, but we are beginning further back along the lake which is far too attractive to leave unexplored.

Lake Constance (Bodensee)
This huge lake is not all in Germany; part of the south-western shore is in Switzerland and the south-eastern corner is Austrian. It is forty-five miles long and up to nine miles wide, almost an inland sea, with fleets of ferry boats, a myriad of yachts and pleasure boats and warm clear water – pure enough in its deeper areas to be used in nearby towns and piped to *Stuttgart* over 90 miles away. The whole area is known for its mild climate and plentiful sunshine. With

orchards sloping down to the water and its colourful villages and busy tourist centres, it is a very popular holiday destination. It may well be that you will be unable to drag yourself away and decide to spend your whole vacation here. There is plenty to see and do in the immediate area.

Konstanz and the Rhine Falls

The *Rhine* enters the lake at its southernmost end near *Bregenz* in Austria and leaves it as a narrow channel connecting the *Bodensee* with a smaller lake, known as the *Untersee*, near *Konstanz*, a German town on the western side of the lake almost surrounded by Switzerland. From *Konstanz* it is a short trip to the famous Rhine Falls at *Schaffhausen* just across the border in Switzerland. There is a promenade below the Falls with a magnificent view of the foaming water, 490 feet wide dropping with a thunderous noise from a height of seventy feet.

Mainau Island

Another favourite excursion from *Konstanz* is to *Mainau* Island in the branch of the lake known as *Überlingersee*. This island is famous for its flowers, palms and orange trees and is very popular with visitors. The island is owned by Count Bernadotte of Sweden who lives in the three-winged castle. You can get to the island either by ferry boat from *Konstanz* or by walking across the small footbridge north of the city.

Meersburg

A car ferry will take you across the lake to *Meersburg*, one of those gems of medieval architecture which has survived and been lovingly preserved. Unfortunately, it is now threatened by its own success as, during the day, it is invaded by hundreds of tourists wandering around the steep streets, admiring the half-timbered houses (many covered in climbing plants and the inevitable window-boxes full of flowers), the fountains and the oldest castle in Germany — or simply sitting outside one of the old waterfront taverns watching the world go by.

Friedrichshafen and the Zeppelins

Travel further southeastwards down the lakeside and you will reach *Friedrichshafen*, the second largest town on *Lake Constance*, famous in aeronautical history as the birthplace of the *Zeppelin*. The very interesting museum devoted to the rise and fall of the airships is well worth a visit and there is a pleasantly wide promenade to stroll along. The lake is at its widest here and, perhaps strangely, it is from this point that you can get a ferry across to *Romanshorn* in Switzerland.

Langenargen, Nonnenhorn and Wasserburg

Further down the lakeside from *Friedrichshafen* are a number of small towns and villages which are favourite holiday spots. *Langenargen* is a charming town with an attractive tree lined promenade and a castle. *Nonnenhorn* is smaller with a pretty town square and lakeside walks among fruit trees and vineyards. One of the most beautiful spots is *Wasserburg*, squashed onto a narrow tongue of land jutting out into the lake. It has a baroque church with an onion shaped tower, a castle which has been turned into a luxury hotel and a most helpful Tourist Office where the young lady on duty, unable to find us a room when we arrived late in the evening, took us home to her mother's farmhouse and installed us in a lovely room under the eaves.

Lindau

From the *Wasserburg* peninsula you will get your first view of the most famous place on *Lake Constance, Lindau*, an island which seems to be floating on the lake and moored to the shore by two narrow bridges.

Most visitors come by ferryboat, arriving at the harbour whose entrance is guarded by two monuments; an enormous sculpted Bavarian Lion on one side and, on the other, the so-called New Lighthouse. The "old" lighthouse, on the quayside, dates from the thirteenth century and is known as the *Mangturm*. After strolling round the harbour area, explore the walled town with its narrow, twisting streets lined with picturesque old houses and inns. If it is a clear day you will get an unparalleled view of the lake with its background of mountains — perhaps the peaks of The Three Sisters in nearby *Liechtenstein*. At night, the lake becomes a fairyland of lights, the casino opens and if you are not one of the lucky ones staying on the island, you can return to the mainland with a romantic trip on one of the white steamers.

Across the border to Bregenz

The famous Alpine Road, known as the *Alpenstrasse*, starts from *Lindau* but before setting out on the rest of your journey you might enjoy a trip just across the border to *Bregenz* in Austria where each summer an extravagant open-air production of a musical or light opera is presented. In a large open-air auditorium, the front row of stalls is right on the edge of the shore and the huge and spectacular stage is some yards away "floating" on the lake. Check with the Austrian Tourist Office for dates of performances. It is a magical experience not to be missed if you are in the area at the right time — usually the end of July and beginning of August.

The health resorts of the Westallgäu

The *Alpenstrasse* leaves *Lindau* going northward as the B308, a wide sweeping road which curves through the outskirts of the *Bregenzerwald* (Bregenz forest) close to a series of small health resorts, such as *Scheidegg* and *Simmerberg*, where visitors can enjoy fishing and swimming in the forest lakes in summer and skiing in the winter. Some of the villages have mineral springs, others rely on their healthy climate.

Oberstaufen

Oberstaufen also offers a "kur" — in this case a type of controlled fast which is supposed to clear the body of impurities but which is enlivened by the drinking not of medicinal waters but of *Glühwein*! There are excellent walks in the area and a cable car lift to the summit of the *Hochgrat* (6008ft high). In the country areas nearby, in the summer months, there is a festival known as a *Bergmesse* which starts with a religious service on a hill-top and continues with beer, sausages and bands for singing and dancing. The people around here are keen to keep local traditions alive so watch out for other festivities such as folklore festivals with *Schuhplattler* dancers and Alpine horn players.

Winter sports centres

Continuing along the *Alpenstrasse*, you pass through several more small summer and winter resorts such as *Thalkirchdorf* and *Immenstadt* and arrive in *Sonthofen*, a centre for summer and winter sports with an open-all-year camp site. A little way south is *Fischen im Allgäu* which in addition to the usual tourist attractions also has an open-air pool naturally heated from the depths of the earth so that it is possible to swim in its steaming waters well into December. The *Alpenstrasse* skirts the Austrian border passing through small resorts such as *Hindelang, Oberjoch* and *Nesselwang* which welcome both summer and winter visitors, to reach *Füssen*, already mentioned as the finishing point of the *Romantic Road*.

King Ludwig's castles

From *Füssen* a detour must be made to visit the Royal castles of *Hohenschwangau* and *Neuschwanstein. Hohenschwangau* is the "old" castle although it only dates back to 1832 when the present neo-Gothic style building was created on the site of a thirteenth century ruin. Built for Maximilian II the state rooms are highly decorated with large murals depicting sagas and legends which are said to have influenced Wagner, a frequent visitor as a guest of Maximilian's son, later to be better known as Mad King Ludwig. There are, of course, splendid views from the terraces especially of *Schloss Neuschwanstein*, a fairy tale castle which is surely the most photographed and well known in Germany. The original plan was sketched by a theatrical designer for Ludwig and inspired by the operas of Wagner. Both castles are open to the public at stated times with guided tours in many languages which are extremely popular – *Neuschwanstein* alone attracts over a million visitors each year – so you may wish to arrange

129

your visit to avoid the busiest times. If you are not too exhausted after your tour, walk up the Pollat Gorge to the *Marienbrücke* which spans the ravine and provides the best general view of the castle and its surroundings.

Joining the Romantic Road or visiting Linderhof

At this point in your journey the official *Alpine Road* joins the route of the *Romantic Road* as far as *Steingaden*. You might prefer to cross into Austria to join the 314 to *Reutte* and then back across the border to visit another of Ludwig's castles. Said to be his favourite, *Linderhof*, is a small cream coloured palace built deep in the forest in imitation of the style of Louis XIV. It is set in a beautifully laid-out park which includes a grotto with a tiny lake, a Moorish pavilion and waterfalls which lead to a Neptune fountain which plays daily each hour from 9am to 5pm when it spouts 104 feet into the air.

Oberammergau

The next important stop will be *Oberammergau*, well worth a visit at any time but invaded by thousands of tourists every ten years — in the years ending with a zero — for the presentation of the Passion Play. Beginning in 1634 as an act of piety to give thanks for relief from the plague, the play now involves 1,500 local people and lasts five and a half hours. It is performed many times between mid-May and the end of September in an open air arena which has 4,800 seats and which is open to visitors in the years when the performances do not take place. You will also be able to see the painted houses — look out for pictures of Red Riding Hood and Hansel and Gretel — and buy, or at least admire, some of the many woodcarvings for which the town is famous. It even has an international school of woodcarving.

There are many kilometres of walking paths, some level and relaxing, others more strenuous and leading to the mountain tops, all well kept and clearly marked. Or you can ride on the cabin or chair-lifts up to the peaks to appreciate the magnificent views the lazy way. On the way up or down you can stop for some good food in the traditional mountain huts. There is also a heated "Wave-Mountain Pool". In winter there is cross-country skiing available including the famous "King Ludwig Round Course" and the cabin, chair and tow lifts take enthusiasts up to fantastic skiing areas. For the less ambitious there is tobogganing, horse-sleigh riding or simply winter-walking on the well-kept tracks.

Ettal and the Loisach valley

Nearby, the baroque Benedictine monastery at *Ettal* dominates its village which consists of a few houses and shops which sell the *Ettal Klosterlikor* made by the monks from twenty-six different alpine herbs.

The road then climbs up through a series of hair-pin bends before descending again into the *Loisach* valley to *Garmisch-Partenkirchen*.

Garmisch-Partenkirchen

Another example of twin towns which have joined to provide this 21-letter place name, *Garmisch—Partenkirchen* has many claims to fame. It is the metropolis of the Bavarian Alps and a great international winter resort but it retains a small town atmosphere and you may still see local people wearing traditional costumes.

The Winter Olympics were held there in 1936 and provided the town with an enormous Ski Stadium — with room for 100,000 spectators; two Olympic ski jump platforms — one 240 feet and a smaller 180 feet — and a special jump for learners; an Olympic Ice Stadium which contains three rinks; and an indoor swimming pool with a wave-making machine as well as an outdoor pool.

For those more interested in history and architecture, there is a row of fine houses around the *Marienplatz*. The home of the composer Richard Strauss who lived here until his death in 1949 can be visited and there are several old churches and museums worth a visit.

131

Up the Zugspitze

The outstanding excursion is to the summit of the *Zugspitze*. You can travel most of the way up by an hour-long ride in a modern cog-wheel train followed by a four-minute cable-car trip or more speedily by a cable-railway from *Eibsee*. There is a modern hotel built right into the side of the mountain — a fantastic view and a memorable experience — if you can afford it!

Another interesting excursion starts with a cable-car ride followed by a walk through the *Partnachklamm*, a steep gorge where tunnels and galleries lead past waterfalls and a rushing mountain stream.

Mittenwald

A detour of twelve miles from *Garmisch-Partenkirchen* will bring you to the village of *Mittenwald*, famous for its violin-making which started when a local man returned home after learning the art from Stradivari. There are still six violin makers living in the village and a museum which is devoted to the trade. There are photogenic painted houses with overhanging eaves and a baroque church covered with frescoes as well as spa facilities and beautifully landscaped gardens. Choose from nearly sixty miles of walking trails winding into the hills or take the two-stage chairlift up the nearby *Karwendel* and *Wetterstein* ranges.

Along the Isar valley

Back on the Alpine Road, you will travel through rolling meadows to *Wallgau*, a small village surrounded by mountains. Not far away is Germany's highest lake, the *Walchensee*, 2630 feet up in the mountains. The road then becomes the B307 winding along the river to the *Sylvenstein-Stausee* reservoir which drowned an old village called *Fall* which has been rebuilt on a slope above the lake. The road crosses the lake on a modern viaduct and then goes into and out of Austria through the *Achen Pass*.

Kreuth

We then follow the *Grosser Weissach* to the small winter sport resort of *Kreuth*. Nearby at *Wildbad Kreuth* is an isolated spa hotel surrounded by steep mountains where Czar Nicholas I once took the waters which still flow into fountains in the foyer. There is a cable-car station which will take experienced mountain walkers on a difficult hike in summer and in winter, high-alpine skiers up to the summit.

Tegernsee

At *Rottach-Egern* you will see the *Tegernsee*, set in a picture-book landscape with banks which are almost exclusively privately owned by Germany's jet-set. *Rottach-Egern* at the south and *Gmund* at the northern end are winter and summer resorts with the lake providing sport for either ice-skaters or yachtsmen while *Bad Wiessee* on the west bank is a health spa specialising in chloride, iodine and sulphuric springs and with a modern covered promenade and a music pavilion.

The road circles the lake and will take you to all these and to *Tegernsee* town. Just south of *Gmund* is the road to another lake, the *Schliersee*, where you rejoin the 307 and go on to the village of *Bayrischzell*, one of the most attractive and popular winter and summer resorts on the Alpine Road. It is a centre for many excellent walks and ski slopes.

Tatzelwurm

The road becomes spectacular after *Bayrischzell*, climbing steeply up a series of hairpin bends. Just off the main road is a waterfall in a dark gorge called *Tatzelwurm* where legend says a dragon used to bar the way.

The Inn Valley

Here the road turns north to *Deggendorf*, with its chalet balconies full of flowers, then joins the motorway system (A93/E45 northbound and then the A8/E52 eastbound) until reaching *Bernau* at the foot of the 5475-foot *Kampenwand*.

Chiemsee

Bernau is a small rural resort which welcomes visitors who enjoy its setting close to *Chiemsee*, the largest lake in *Bavaria*, surrounded by green pastures and a background of mountains. They have facilities for swimming – either in the lake or in a new indoor pool; for wind-surfing; tennis and squash; and cable-cars which travel up into the heights. The lake, of course, attracts thousands of visitors for long and short stays. The people of Munich come down the motorway at weekends while visitors from further afield come to camp in the numerous sites around the lake or to stay in the many excellent *Gasthofen* and hotels in the area. The fishing is excellent with bream, pike, eel and trout and naturalists can look out for almost 250 types of birds and many different plant species. **DER Travel Service** have a "Nature Lover's Holiday" here with travel arranged by rail or air as you prefer. It is centred at *Prien* in the southwest corner of the lake. The town centre is about half a mile from the waterside with an interesting *Hiematmuseum* and art gallery. On the lakeside is the town's harbour where ferries leave for other resorts around the lake and to two small islands. On the smaller island, *Fraueninsel*, is a Benedictine convent, founded in the eighth century, now used as a boarding school. On the larger island, *Herrenchiemsee*, is Ludwig's largest and last palace. It was the building and fitting out of this that finally made him bankrupt. Tourists can visit the island to walk in the palace gardens or, during the summer, to listen to concerts in the candle-lit "Hall of Mirrors", to eat in the restaurant or even to stay in part of the building which is now a hotel.

South to Reit im Winkl

Leaving the lake, the road continues through fairly flat country to *Grassau* and *Marquartstein*, a village resort which keeps up the old traditions with a folk theatre and where local costumes are often worn on Sundays and feast days.

After *Marquartstein*, the scenery becomes more mountainous through *Unterwössen* and *Oberwössen* with their pretty lake *Wössnersee*, beautiful but cold for swimming as it is fed by streams straight from the mountains. The road now passes through a narrow gorge and arrives close to *Reit im Winkl*, an attractive peaceful village filled with flowers in summer which becomes the hub of activity in the winter when it is a well known skiing centre reputed to have the heaviest snowfalls in Bavaria. The village stands at a height of 2,500 feet and is surrounded by mountains and forests with paths for rambles and hikes of all grades. For summer visitors there are indoor and outdoor swimming pools, small lakes for boating and bathing, and facilities for tennis, rock-climbing and mini-golf. There is even a new nine-hole golf course. Only a mile or two from the Austrian border, *Reit* is in an ideal place for a trip across the border or a two-country holiday.

We pass four lakes with facilities for bathing and wind-surfing, a nature reserve and several pretty villages on the way to the next resort *Ruhpolding*. It is actually a few miles north of the *Alpenstrasse* on a road which connects with the motorway south of *Chiemsee* and which provides a quicker and less scenic route if you are short of time and wish to miss the *Bernau* to *Reit* section of the road.

If there are children in the party the detour to *Ruhpolding* will be essential in order to visit the *Märchenfamilienpark* (The fairy tale park) where they can meet models of many fairy tale characters including Snow White and the Seven Dwarfs, Hansel and Gretel and the Sleeping Beauty. They will also enjoy rides on ponies or a miniature train and exploring a miniature town. And there is the *Märchenwald* (an enchanted forest) with well-signposted woodland walks.

The glacier garden

Back on the B305 you come to the *Gletschergarten* (the glacier garden). Use the parking places on either side of the road to stop and walk up the steps which have been cut into the hillside to allow visitors to view the result of this massive geological upheaval which probably occurred some 20,000 years ago.

Berchtesgadenerland

Turning off the 305 on a minor road past a delightful lake *Thumsee*, we reach *Bad Reichenhall*, an elegant spa town famous for its salt deposits. Visitors can take the waters, tour the old salt workings, or stroll in the parks and botanical gardens. From here you can take the B20 direct to *Berchtesgaden* or the B21 and then back on the B305 to arrive in the same place by a more interesting and circuitous route. This leads past the *Saalachsee*, a long narrow lake, up the *Schwarzbachwacht Pass* through dramatic scenery, with densely wooded valleys and the peaks of the *Reiter Alp*. Here there is a wonderful view down into *Ramsau*, a village popular with both painters and climbers. There is a small cream church near a mountain stream crossed by a rustic bridge. It is the church in which the composer of Silent Night was once the priest. There are views of the *Watzmann* and the *Hochkalter* which artists struggle to re-create and mountaineers to climb.

The spectacular mountain scenery leads to the *Nationalpark Berchtesgaden*, an area of about 460 sq km with protected wildlife including chamois, deer, ibex and, in the higher mountains, marmots. In the centre of the park is one of the loveliest lakes in Bavaria, the *Königsee*, on which you can ride – or rather glide – in an electrically powered boat silently over the dark, still waters.

Berchtesgaden

Originally an old market town, *Berchtesgaden* was built on such a rocky and wooded site it is as high as it is wide. There is a castle-palace and a Romanesque and Gothic church. A favourite visit is to the *Salzmuseum* where visitors don protective clothing to travel astride an old mining train through high caverns before walking down steps or sliding down a chute to a grotto bright with coloured salt crystals. A film show is followed by a second slide down a chute, which leads to an underground salt lake which is crossed on a raft to another sparkling grotto, followed by a lift to the train ride back to the fresh air. Not a trip to be undertaken by the claustrophobic!

The other popular visit is to Hitler's house — the "Eagle's Nest". Most of the building was destroyed at the end of the war but its fantastic setting is still to be seen. Part of the out-buildings are used by the Alpine Club as a mountain *Gaststätte*.

The end of the road

The Alpine Road ends here in this famous resort which is so busy that it has become one of the most expensive places in Bavaria, so you would probably be wise to find somewhere in the surrounding area if you plan to stay for a while. A few miles away, over the Austrian border, is one of the great European cities which it would be a pity to miss. A visit to *Salzburg* is a "must" for those who have not been there. You will then be back on the motorway system and ready to start your journey home.

CHAPTER SEVENTEEN:
TO THE HARZ MOUNTAINS

This journey will take you through the heartland of Germany's heavy industry — the *Ruhr* — and then into attractive yet relatively unknown holiday areas to reach the beautiful *Weser* valley and the *Harz* mountains on the border with East Germany.

The Lower Rhine Valley

Crossing the Dutch border south of *Arnhem* you will be in the Lower Rhine Valley where the countryside is still Dutch looking, flat with windmills and small red brick towns. The Rhine, as ever, is busy with barges taking cargoes out to the sea at *Rotterdam*. Several of the small towns are well worth a visit. *Kleve*, just nine miles south of the Dutch border, is an attractive small resort town which was the home town of Anne of Cleves, the fourth wife of Henry VIII. Look out as you pass through *Kalkar* for the marketplace with its brick houses, turreted town hall and an old lime tree under which cases were once tried. Many people stop here to see the beautifully carved altarpieces in the church of St. Nicholas.

Then *Xanten* is well worth a stop to visit the excavated Roman fortress and amphitheatre which are being restored to look as much as possible as they did 2000 years ago. The amphitheatre is used for modern theatrical productions — they were presenting "*West Side Story*" the week after our last visit — and there is a Roman games room where you can sit and play reconstructed versions of some of the games played by Roman soldiers to pass the time during their off duty periods. Purists may not care for this use of archeological remains but for those of us less knowledgeable — and particularly for children — it certainly brings the past to life.

The Ruhr

It is then across the *Rhine* and into the outskirts of the *Ruhr*, where six million people live and work in the greatest industrial area in Europe. It is made up of many towns and villages which have merged together so that, as you travel through, it is difficult to know where one ends and another begins. If this is a holiday visit you will probably prefer to go onto the network of motorways and get an overall view as you drive through. If you decide to stop, however, you will find that many of the smaller towns along the *Ruhr* river have interesting ruins, half-timbered houses and castles among the forested hills and reservoirs where leisure resorts with facilities for sports and other activities have been created. In the larger towns, such as *Essen*, there are plenty of theatres, orchestras and museums as well as cultural events and festivals. *Dortmund* on the eastern side of the *Ruhr* conurbation is famous for its beer. Its seven breweries produce more than ten per cent of the enormous beer output of the country and some can be visited by applying to: **Verband Dortmunder Bierbrauer, Karl-Marx-Strasse 56, D-4600 Dortmund**. The town is also proud of its tall TV tower with rotating restaurant and a sports hall which appears to be made entirely of glass.

The Sauerland

South-east of *Dortmund* is the *Sauerland*. This is an area very popular with the inhabitants of the *Ruhr* towns and with Dutch and Belgian visitors. But it is virtually unknown to the British. The hills are actually a number of green plateaux cut by deep forested valleys containing many lakes, some now used as reservoirs. There are small towns and villages where accommodation of all kinds, including farmhouses, self-catering, hostels and bed and breakfast, is readily available and comparatively inexpensive. There are facilities for swimming in the lakes or in the many indoor and outdoor swimming pools, sailing, windsurfing and, of course, boat trips. Riding, cycling and tennis are readily available and there is even a winter sports centre around the villages of *Winterberg* and *Alt-Astenberg* near the highest mountain in the area, the 2,760 foot high *Kahler Asten*. It is an area for wandering either on foot — there are plenty of waymarked footpaths — or by car.

If you enter the area from *Dortmund* there is an attractive road — the B236 — which follows the *Lenne* valley south and east to the high mountains of the *Rothaargebirge*. *Althena*, one of the first small towns you come to, is not particularly attractive but it has a castle which was the world's first youth hostel and now houses a museum showing the history of youth hostelling and rambling. About ten miles east is a holiday area around the town of *Balve* where there are spectacular caves which were homes for prehistoric man. These are now used for various events including an annual jazz festival and shooting contest. A short detour off this route will take you further south to the *Ebbegebirge Naturpark* with the *Biggersee*, the largest reservoir in the area which has five recognized bathing beaches, water sports facilities and lake cruises. Nearby are the *Attahöhle* stalactite caves. On the way up the *Kahler Asten* there are attractive mountain villages — as well as slate quarries! — and a splendid view from the top.

The Eder Dam and the Waldeck region

Leaving the *Sauerland* and travelling east there is a small forested region around the river *Eder* which is becoming popular with tourists.

From the terrace of the castle at *Waldeck* there is a fine view of the lake which is formed by the *Eder Dam*. It was completed in 1914 and breached by the RAF in 1943 as commemorated in the book and film *The Dambusters*. The bombing caused catastrophic floods but the wall of the dam was repaired and re-instated and I defy anyone to "see the join"! There are boat trips on the lake including one to the interesting and attractive *Wildpark* on the other bank.

Bad Wildungen

Bad Wildungen is a spa town with medicinal waters said to be beneficial for diseases of the kidney and gall bladder. It is a very wealthy place with an attractive modern *Kurhaus*.

Visitors to the spa have their own glass mugs kept at a counter in the horseshoe-shaped entrance hall to the *Trinkhalle* where there are several exclusive shops. There are acres of well kept gardens which contain flowering plants from all over the world and plenty of comfortable seats placed throughout the grounds and buildings. Wealthy patients can sit and listen to the orchestra playing in one of the two bandstands or play outdoor chess while they sip the foul-tasting water or wait for their massage appointments.

Fritzlar

Fritzlar on the river *Eder* is a photogenic old town with a medieval centre where multi-coloured half-timbered houses, some covered with wooden shingles, surround the market square.

Kassel

This too is an old town but much of its historic centre was destroyed by bombing in World War II. Nowadays it is an important industrial centre which covers a wide area and has a population of over a quarter of a million. It is known as a city of gardens with many parks, traffic-free promenades and subways to keep pedestrians away from the cars and lorries.

A few miles out of town is the *Schloss Wilhelmhöhe*, an eighteenth century palace in a huge park with baroque temples, grottos, fountains, bridges and an aqueduct. At the summit is the gigantic Hercules Statue and a vista across the park and the castle to the town below.

Inside, the castle is richly furnished and houses an art gallery to which entrance is free. It contains many very fine

Old Masters including one of the largest Rembrandt collections in the world as well as paintings by Dürer, Rubens, Van Dyck and Franz Hals and others. On the ground floor there is an important museum of Greek and Roman sculptures.

Modern art is also appreciated in *Kassel*. The *Documenta*, an international exhibition of contemporary art, considered to be the world's largest art exhibition, is held in the town every four years. And there is a Brothers Grimm Museum which illustrates the life and works of the brothers who learned and collected many of their stories roundabout.

Weserbergland

Considered to be one of the loveliest rivers in Germany, the *Weser* valley is also renowned for its fairy tales and legends.

The first town, *Hannoversch Münden*, was built on two islands where two rivers meet to become the *Weser*. It is an extremely picturesque town. Its hundreds of half-timbered, carved and painted houses built between the sixteenth and eighteenth centuries are well preserved. There is also a very fine Town Hall and the remains of the city walls.

The B80 follows the river north from *Hannoversch Münden*. It is known as the *Deutsche Märchenstrasse* (the German Fairy Tale Road) as it was in this area that the Grimm Brothers collected many of their famous stories. At *Veckerhagen*, a picturesque village eight miles up the valley, you can cross the river by an old ferry. Or turn west on a side road to visit *Sababurg*, a small and partly ruined castle on the top of a hill which is reputed to have been the inspiration for the Sleeping Beauty's castle. It is sometimes used for open-air performances of suitably romantic plays. Back on the B80 on the west bank of the river you will come to *Bad Karlshafen*, a lovely white spa town built on a uniform plan with baroque buildings. Then through *Beverungen* and *Höxter* to *Hölzminden*. From here, you could return to *Hannoversch Münden* down the other bank of the river or cut across country straight to the *Harz* region, leaving the rest of the Weser valley, including *Bad Pyrmont* and *Hamelin*, for your return journey.

The Harz Mountains

These wooded hills covering 785 square miles have a tradition of mining — once gold and silver, nowadays zinc, lead and barium oxide. The highest point, the *Brocken*, is actually across the border in East Germany. It is a holiday area particularly popular with Danes who come to see the mountains and the villages with their attractive painted houses. It has high rainfall and plenty of snow so that the forests in summer are always green and the highest areas become skiing centres in winter. It is a small compact area which can be explored at your leisure and has plenty of inexpensive accommodation in many of the small resorts and spas.

Osterode at the western edge is a walled town with some fine fifteenth and seventeenth century buildings grouped round a wide square called the *Kornmarkt*. North of *Osterode* is a small spa called *Bad Grund* where, among other facilities for visitors, is an English Tearoom run by a friendly English couple who have a few rooms to let as well as providing delicious tea and cakes. Up in the hills are many small resort towns including *Braunlage, Claustal-Zellerfield, St. Andreasberg* where you can tour an old silver mine, *Altenau, Herzberg am Harz, Lautenthal im Oberhärz, Schulenberg* and *Wolfshagen im Harz*. In any of these, you could have a quiet holiday, walking or relaxing in beautiful surroundings. There are also dozens of spas which offer cures of all kinds as well as facilities for ordinary holiday activities. *Bad Harzberg* is very near the border with East Germany, and is beautifully situated with a chair lift to take you to the top of the *Grosse Burgberg* for a walk in summer or for skiing in winter.

Goslar

"If you think you have seen everything possible in the way of medieval towns, you are likely to revise your ideas" says Fodor. "A mining town near the Harz mountains" says Michelin. Both, believe it or not are talking about *Goslar*, the most ancient and interesting town in the Harz region and one which is best savoured by a stroll around on foot. The lead and silver mines which created the wealth of *Goslar* in the Middle Ages are still there but it is the town built for the workers and other inhabitants of that time and later which draws visitors today. Street after street of houses built from the fifteenth to the nineteenth century in all the different styles favoured during those times – Gothic, Renaissance, baroque. There are houses with carved timber fronts, with tall gables, with slate shingles arranged in intricate patterns as well as magnificent fifteenth and sixteenth century guildhouses, several twelfth century churches and an old Romanesque palace that once belonged to the German Emperors. In the old Town Hall in the market place, is a room whose walls and ceiling were entirely covered with paintings by an unknown artist in 1500. These have been carefully preserved to retain their bright colours. A place to wander and enjoy.

Starting back

Before you start your journey west try to find time for a detour north to three towns, each of which is worth a visit in its own right.

Brunswick (Braunschweig)

This is a famous old city which was largely destroyed in World War II. The market place and the old castle square have been authentically restored and the rebuilt city is one of the success stories of the German economic miracle, having developed as a modern industrial town making buses and other large vehicles, photographic equipment and cans for food preservation.

Celle

This beautiful old city, on the other hand, was virtually undamaged and still looks like something out of a picture book. The ancient half-timbered houses have stepped gables and carved beams and the town has the peaceful atmosphere of earlier times.

Hanover

Turning south-west on the B3 brings you to *Hanover*. For just over a century the rulers of *Hannover* (the German spelling) also became the kings of England where for some reason one of the "n"s was dropped. The city today is still the capital of Lower Saxony (*Niedersachsen*) and although it has lost much of its political influence, it has become an important hub of industry and commerce. The centre of the city has been skilfully restored with a large pedestrianised double-decker shopping mall and several attractive parks and tree-lined streets. The most famous park, the *Herrenhausen*, is well worth a visit. There is a maze of walks and flower-beds studded with fountains, the largest of which shoots jets of water nearly 300 feet into the air. The park also has the world's only existing hedge-theatre which is still used today not only for Shakespeare, Molière and Brecht but also for ballet and jazz concerts. On the other side of the road is the smaller botanical garden with large greenhouses where rare orchids are grown. Sensibly they provide stools in each greenhouse so that visitors can sit in comfort while they study or photograph the plants.

Hamelin

Back on the banks of the *Weser* we come to another town whose name has been anglicized, this time by adding an "i". *Hamelin (Hameln)* is an attractive town which would be worth visiting to see its colourful carved houses. But it also has the unique association of the Pied Piper story, an old legend immortalized by *Goethe* and in English, by Robert Browning. On Sundays between 12 and 12.30 the famous story is re-enacted on a large stage in front of an unusual building called the Wedding House (*Hochzeithaus*).

Bad Pyrmont

A short distance further south-west is *Bad Pyrmont*, a fashionable and well-known watering place. It has one of the most beautiful spa parks in Germany with many species of palm tree and artistically arranged vistas. In a beautiful setting among the hills of the Upper Weser, its mild climate and mineral springs are said to be beneficial to skin diseases and blood circulation problems. The many cafés and restaurants spread their white spa chairs and tables out into the wide street alongside the park and visitors can spend happy hours sitting watching the world pass by. During one visit we made, the town was especially busy as it was the day of the parade of the area *Schutzvereine*, the shooting clubs, who vie with each other in the magnificence of their bemedalled uniforms and banners, the precision of their marching and the volume of sound produced by their bands.

Münster

By now it will probably be time to start making your way home. A good place for last-minute shopping would be the *Westphalian* capital, *Münster*. In the centre of a wooded plain, it is a large agricultural market town. The *Principalmarkt* is the busiest street with elegant houses which have been cleverly restored.

Accidental discoveries

On the way, if your map-reading is as inefficient as mine is sometimes, you may come across a small gem of a place called *Schwalenberg* which we discovered by accident. It is a quiet village with beautiful old houses and an old church where life seems to carry on as it was a hundred years ago. No doubt you will make discoveries of your own. One of the best and most interesting parts of a tour of this kind is the unexpected and unplanned diversion.

Part Three:
Holidays without a car

CHAPTER EIGHTEEN:
FLYING VISITS

Enjoy the excitement of Carnival in *Cologne*. Marvel at the modern architecture in *Stuttgart*. Tour the beer cellars in *Munich* or the *Reeperbahn* in *Hamburg*. Go shopping for clothes in *Düsseldorf* or toys in *Nuremberg*. A good way to sample life in Germany would be a short break in one of the large cities or towns. Several companies offer breaks which include flight and quality accommodation in Germany's interesting cities.

Cologne (Köln)

The capital of the Rhineland, *Cologne* is one of Germany's major cities. Its massive cathedral, which miraculously survived the intense bombing of the city during World War II, has a Gothic façade with gables and spires which rise to 515ft. This is over 100 feet taller than the spire of Salisbury cathedral. It has some magnificent fourteenth century stained glass windows, intricately carved choir stalls with 104 seats and ornately decorated and intricately painted altars and shrines.

It is unquestionably the heart of the city both spiritually and geographically. Wherever you wander around the pedestrianised shopping streets or in the old town centre, you will be able to see the twin towers guiding you back. Around its square are the railway station, the museums, hotels and shopping streets and not far away, the bridges crossing the everbusy *Rhine*.

There are guided coach tours through the city if you wish,

but with its compact city centre, *Cologne* is easily explorable on foot. If you wish to travel further afield there are plenty of cream-coloured taxis and an excellent public transport system. There are many stores and shops close to the centre selling crafts such as pottery and leatherwork and you will no doubt wish to buy its most famous product — Eau de Cologne — the French name of which has stuck since the time of Napoleon. There are lots of excellent eating places and you may be tempted to try the local delicacy *Himmel und Erde* (Heaven and Earth), a combination of apples, blood-sausage and leeks. For evening entertainment, you could visit one of the theatres, the opera house or one or more of the many nightclubs or bars, some of which have live popular music. There are nine municipal and several private museums, an art gallery, a new concert hall and numerous parks. The Rhine Park, which has a specially provided open-air dancing area around a fountain, is near the modern Trade Fair Centre which welcomes business visitors from all over the world to conventions, conferences and exhibitions.

Cologne is well worth a visit at any time of the year but to experience the city and its inhabitants in most uninhibited mood you must be there at Carnival time — the weekend before Shrove Tuesday. Carnival is celebrated with enthus-iasm in several parts of Germany and particularly in the Rhineland area. But *Cologne* has the largest, longest, noisiest and most exciting procession and every citizen and visitor is involved in the enjoyment. The weather may be cold but the atmosphere is warm with friendliness and pleasure.

Düsseldorf

Düsseldorf played a big part in what has become known as "the German economic miracle" and is now responsible for about ten per cent of its foreign trade. Düsseldorfers earn more than the national average and their wealth has allowed the much bombed city to be restored and refurbished to a high standard. It claims to have the Rhineland's smartest and most attractive shopping centre with the most fashion con-scious citizens. The heart of the city is the main street, the long wide *Königsallee*, which runs along both sides of a canal lined with trees. One side houses modern office blocks and banking institutions, the other is lined with exclusive fashion shops, jewellers and boutiques and is the place to buy − and show off − fine clothes. You can sit at one of the pavement cafés watching the *Radschläger*, young lads who make their pocket money and entertain the tourists by cartwheeling up and down the street. At the northern end of the *Kö*, as the residents call it, is the Triton Fountain and the *Hofgarten*, a large park with fountains and statues among the trees and flower gardens.

Düsseldorf has a tradition as a major arts centre and there are important collections of nineteenth century and modern art. For evening entertainment there are plenty of bars and restaurants in the *Altstadt* and more sophisticated nightclubs in the *Königsallee* area. There is usually opera or ballet at the *Deutsche Oper am Rhein* and plays at the *Schauspielhaus*. In the autumn and winter there are concerts in the *Tonhalle* beside the Rhine and at the *Robert Schumann Saal* and sometimes rock concerts in the *Philips-Halle*.

For a few days shopping and high living you could do little better than Düsseldorf − but remember that most shops close on Saturday afternoons if you are thinking of a weekend visit.

Frankfurt

Another showcase of German recovery. Frankfurt has developed from a smallish provincial city into a centre of German business and the hub of its communications network. It is the geographical centre of the Federal Republic and it is said that every conurbation in Europe is within 600 miles of the city. Its airport handles more freight than any other in Europe and its railway station is the largest in Germany. It is also a financial centre, the home of the *Bundesbank* and over 200 other banks, so is sometimes nicknamed "Bankfurt". The *Messe* is a major venue for international trade fairs.

A few years ago *Frankfurt* was voted "Europe's most boring city" and one that most of its inhabitants would prefer to move away from. However, its image is rapidly changing.

149

It has some of the tallest buildings in Europe with more being built. The hotels are of remarkably high standard and their restaurants, particularly some of the out-of-town establishments, are considered to offer good value for money.

For sight-seeing, there is a converted old tram which travels a circular route and can be boarded at any point. *Frankfurt* is on the river *Main* and there are several bridges crossing the river which will take you to the amusement district known as *Alt Sachsenhausen* or to some interesting museums. The *Städelsches Kunstinstitut* has an impressive art collection, and the *Liebieghaus* has a world-class collection of sculpture. There is also a decorative arts museum – the *Museum für Kunsthandwerk* – in a beautifully designed new building which houses a collection covering work from the Middle Ages to Art Nouveau, and a *Bundespostmuseum*, a collection of artefacts connected with the postal system.

Out of town there is the Zoological Garden which has over 700 species of animals and is regarded as one of the finest in the world with its *Exotarium* specially designed to re-create suitable living conditions for its inhabitants.

Hamburg

Short breaks in *Hamburg* are available both by air and by sea. *Scandinavian Seaways* advertise cruises and visits of two days or longer. Arriving by boat, you will enjoy what is probably the best approach to *Hamburg*, coming up the river estuary, past the dykes and marshes, through the multitude of small yachts and ships of all sizes. There are excellent views of the rows of fishermen's cottages which are now homes for commuters and then the industrial docklands before the ship berths at a quay in the very heart of the city.

Hamburg was one of the most heavily bombed German cities in the last war with more than half its buildings damaged or destroyed. The rebuilders turned disaster into opportunity and the city has become a showplace for modern architecture with its steel and glass office buildings, underwater tunnels, new bridges and apartment blocks. It has a very efficient public transport system combining a *U-Bahn* (the underground railway system) and a connecting *S-Bahn* (the suburban surface railway).

There is plenty to see and do. Take a boat trip on or a walk around the two *Alster* lakes in the heart of the city. The larger *Aussenalster* and the small *Binnenalster* are joined by two bridges, the Lombard and the John F. Kennedy, and are surrounded by tree-lined avenues and some famous streets and buildings.

To get an overall view of the city, climb or take the lift to the top of the copper tower of St. Michael's church. This is *Hamburg's* most beautiful church, restored before World War I after a fire, and then again after World War II when it suffered serious bomb damage.

A different view is from the rotating restaurant at the top of the 890-foot TV tower called the *Heinrich Hertz Turm*. The shopping streets are well worth exploring and you can hardly miss the opulent *Rathaus* in the *Marktplatz*. This Renaissance, style palace built in 1886, has 647 rooms (six more than Buckingham Palace, I believe), including a fine festival hall, and vaulted ceilings hung with elaborate chandeliers.

Hamburg is famous for its nightlife, most of all in the clubs of the *Reeperbahn*, a street in the harbour area of *St. Pauli.* Here you will find sex shows running continuously from about 7pm to 4am. In the nearby *Hertbertstrasse* the "ladies" sit in the picture windows of houses. Others stroll in the nearby *Grosse Freiheitstrasse* where they are more readily available for conversation!

But there are more restrained forms of entertainment available too. In the *Musikhalle* there are often symphonic concerts and there is the *Hamburgerische Staatsoper*, the modern replacement for the old opera house. There is also the unique *Hansa Theater* behind the railway station which offers a type of variety programme of singers, jugglers, comedians and acrobats which seems to have died out elsewhere. The audience sits in multi-person upholstered benches with a table for food and drink and a good view of the stage.

If you have more time to spare, you could visit the *Hagenbeck Zoo*; or the world famous *Planten und Blomen* Park, a permanent display of rare plants and gardening at its best. On summer evenings you can enjoy "Waterlight" concerts, with fantastic coloured sprays of water that "dance" in time to music. You could also visit some of the many interesting and varied museums or the *Kramers Amtsstuben*, an area of sixteenth century houses for pensioners or even the Fish market on Sunday morning. With the help of the Information Bureau in *Bieberhaus* at the main railway station, you can thoroughly explore this fascinating city.

Munich (München)

This is the favourite city of most Germans and an excellent choice for a short break. The beautifully restored buildings, the wide range of theatres, concert halls, art galleries, restaurants and shops make it a mecca for tourists. The *Altstadt* (old town) has narrow winding streets and buildings dating from the Middle Ages to the Renaissance. It has a pedestrianised area around the *Marienplatz* where you will find the main shopping streets with many restaurants and beer cellars, including the famous *Hofbräuhaus*.

There is a wide variety of entertainment particularly during the festival months of June and July: opera at the *Nationaltheater*, and the *Staatstheater am Gärtnerplatz*, which also sometimes has musicals as does the *Deutsches Theater*. There are plays at the *Residenztheater* and the *Schauspielhaus* and frequent classical music concerts, particularly in the summer months, in the nearby *Schloss Nymphenburg*. There are numerous nightspots frequented mainly by young people. As far as shopping is concerned, *Munich* has plenty to offer, being particularly famous for fashion and antiques.

Hotels are dearer than those in the country areas but even so you should be able to find comfortable and well furnished accommodation in a Pension for less than you would pay in this country. The larger hotels are of a high standard, having been given a boost when Munich hosted the 1972 Olympic Games.

Don't miss a visit to the Olympic Park about 2 miles north of the centre. It is a short drive or you can take the *U-Bahn* (underground railway) to *Olympiazentrum*. You can go up the Olympic Tower in a lift or walk in the Park, the largest sports and recreation centre in Europe. On some days when there are no events taking place, you can go into the Olympic Stadium itself — now home of *FC Bayern München* — and wander round the terraces under the huge tent-like roof made up of acrylic plates covering an area of 75,000 square metres. An eye-opener for those of us used to British stadia such as Wembley and well worth seeing.

If you fancy a visit to the *Oktoberfest*, go at the end of September and book early as the event now attracts over six million people. *Müncheners* also celebrate Carnival, known as *Fasching*, in the period preceding Lent with up to 2000 costume balls and many other events.

Nuremberg (Nürnberg)
Another target of Allied bombing in World War II, *Nuremberg* has been rebuilt, restored and refurbished with a meticulousness and creativity which is well worth exploring and appreciating. Inside the old city walls, which were all that was left of the old town, is an easily walkable centre devoted to shopping and entertainment. *Nuremberg* is considered one of Germany's least expensive shopping centres and is specially famous for its toys. There is even a toy museum — the *Speilzeugmuseum* — a fascinating collection of toys through the ages from dolls and dolls houses to miniature railways and mechanical playthings of all kinds.

An industrial and business centre, *Nuremberg* is the home of some of Germany's major companies such as Adidas and Grundig and has excellent exhibition and conference facilities. The restaurants produce tasty Fraconian food in which freshwater fish feature largely, as do the excellent local sausages. There are plenty of cafés and bars for evening entertainment and *Bayreuth* is just over 50 miles away if you happen to be visiting during the period of the annual Wagner

Festival. The famous *Christkindlmarkt* takes place just before Christmas in the *Hauptmarkt*, the main square.

Stuttgart

Stuttgart is the wealthy capital of *Baden-Württemberg*, the home of the Mercedes car company and the centre of a large and economically buoyant area. In addition to its industrial activity, *Stuttgart* also has several springs which feed mineral water swimming pools and spa facilities. It is a city of parks and gardens and the centre of a large wine-producing area with over 1000 acres of vineyards within the city limits and there are many orchards in the surrounding countryside. Although not as large as some of Germany's other great cities, it considers itself a cultural rival to *Munich* and is justly proud of its ballet company and orchestra.

It is a compact and walkable city with the usual pedestrianised shopping streets around the *Königstrasse* where you will find department stores, shops, restaurants and cafés. Parallel to the *Königstrasse* is a large park, the *Schlossgarten*, where you will find the *Staatstheater*, the home of the famous ballet company. Nearby is the *Staatsgalerie*, with a well regarded art collection, and the *Landesmuseum*. On Tuesdays, Thursdays and Saturdays there is a colourful street market in the *Schillerplatz*. Nearby are the *Altes Schloss* (old castle), a thirteenth century moated castle, and the baroque *Neue Schloss* (new castle), once the home of the Kings of *Baden-Württemberg* and now used for receptions by the government. But *Stuttgart* is also known for its modern architecture including the *Liederhalle*, an asymmetrical wavy-lined building which houses three acoustically impressive concert halls, and the cubic glass State Parliament building in the *Schlossgarten*. There are also housing estates in the suburbs designed by Le Corbusier and Frank Lloyd Wright which are considered worth visiting by other architects.

The list of hotels does not include many of the well known international chains but most are comfortable and well-maintained as usual in Germany. The local delicacies are lighter and less sausage and pickle based than some other parts of the country and there is more emphasis on eggs and cheese including *Zwiebelküchen*, a type of Swabian Quiche Lorraine. There are two restaurants in the 500 foot high television tower. Instead of the beer cellars so famous in *Munich*, *Stuttgart* favours *Weinstuben* (wine bars) which are usually open only in the evenings. Local wines are served from the barrel and they offer local food such as *Maultaschen*, a kind of ravioli, and *Spätzle*, buttered noodles. The best are usually crowded, cheerful and noisy and most are in attractive old buildings.

How to get there

Most of these cities have international airports and it is, of course, possible to make your own way. However, while European air fares are still controlled, you will probably get a better deal by booking through a travel company.

Intasun offers flights and quality accommodation in city hotels in *Cologne, Düsseldorf* and *Munich*.

DER Travel Service include these three as well as *Augsburg, Bremen, Frankfurt, Freiburg, Hamburg, Hanover, Lübeck, Mainz, Regensburg* and *Stuttgart* on their list of destinations for winter holidays. They will arrange two-centre holidays if you wish.

Other companies listed by The German National Tourist Office as offering city breaks or holidays by air include:

Albany Travel (Manchester) Ltd
Angel Travel Ltd
Cresta Holidays
German Tourist Facilities
Globepost Travel Services
Hamilton Travel
Magnum Holidays
Moswin Tours
Pegasus Holidays Ltd
Taber Holidays
The Travel Force

Breaks in the country

For those rich enough to afford it, **Air Foyle Executive Limited** arrange "Escapades", trips by private plane to the Parkhotel Adler in *Hinterzarten* in the Black Forest or to the famous Brenner's Park Hotel in *Baden-Baden*.

For the less seriously rich, companies such as **Angel Travel** and **Arena Travel** list weekend breaks to the Rhine and Mosel Valleys. **Canterbury Travel** include the *Black Forest* and *Garmisch-Partenkirchen* while **DER** go further afield and have holidays by air in many different parts of the country.

Travelling independently, a flight to *Cologne/Bonn* would be a good starting point for a few days on the *Rhine*, exploring the *Sauerland* (see Chapter Seventeen) or the *Eifel Massif* on the west bank of the *Rhine*. This is a popular holiday region for quiet pastimes such as walking and fishing. You could watch the International Show Jumping in *Aachen* or visit the *Nürburgring* for the motor racing — or have a go round the track yourself if there is no meeting on.

Flying into *Stuttgart* would enable you to spend a few days exploring the northern part of the *Black Forest*, while *Munich* is close enough to the *Bavarian Alps* to allow a brief visit to the lakes and mountains.

CHAPTER NINETEEN:
COACH TOURS, CRUISES AND RAIL HOLIDAYS

Coach tours are the most widely available, and probably the cheapest, way of enjoying a holiday in Germany. If you study the **Holiday Digest** leaflet from the German National Tourist Office you will find a large selection of coach tours covering quite a wide area of the country. The Rhine and Mosel valleys are the most popular destinations. At the last count, there were over fifty companies offering coach tours to different parts of this region. As there is plenty of choice, it would be wise to ask a few questions about pick-up points, the amount of time you will spend travelling, as well as your final destination and type of accommodation before deciding which one to book.

In the following list of companies offering coach tours the code letters show the areas likely to be covered. Rhine Valley (R), Mosel Valley (M), The Black Forest (BF), Bavaria (Bav), The Eifel Mountains (Eif), The Romantic Road (RR), the Sauerland (Sau), Lake Constance (Con), Heidelberg (Heid), Hamburg (Ham), Munich (Mun) and the Harz Mountains (H). Some of the tours to the *Harz* area include a visit to Berlin which might be a convenient way of getting there for a brief visit without the bother of dealing with the formalities yourself.

Airsprung Travel Limited   R, M, BF, Ham, Bav
Angela Holidays   R, H
Antler Holidays Limited   R
Applebys Coaches   R, H

Applegates Supreme Coaches   R, M
Arvonia Coaches   R
B & H Travel Services Limited   R
Bakers Dolphin Tours   R
Bebb Travel   R
Breakaways   R
Buckby's Coaches   M
Cavendish Travel (various)
Charnwood Travel Limited   R, M
City Cruiser Holidays Limited   R, M
Club Cantabrica Coaches Limited   R
Club Relax International   R, Bav
Cosmos Tours Limited   R, M
Cotsworld Travel Limited   R, M, Bav
H.E. Craiggs-Wansbeck Coaches   R, M, BF
Crusader Holidays   R, M, BF, Eif
DA Tours   H, RR, Heid
Dalesman Holidays   R
Davidson Travel   R, Ham
Davies Bros. International Tours   R
Dawson and Sanderson   H
Elsey's Tours Limited   R, Sau
Emblings Coaches   R, BF
Epsoms Coaches   R, M, H
Eurotours   M, Ham, Con, Mun
Excelsior Holidays   R, M, RR
Festive Holidays   R, M, BF
Fitzcharles Coaches Limited   R
Gain Travel Experience Limited   R
Galaxy Holidays   R, M, Bav
Galloway Travel Limited   M
Tony Goss Travel   R, M, H
Go Whittle   R
Grand UK Holidays (for the over 55s)   R, M, BF
Halycon Holidays   R
Happy Days Coaches   R, Ham
Harris Coaches   R, BF, Bav
Harrison Holidays   R, Eif

Holidays Coach (East Kent, Maidstone and District) R, BF
Hoverland European Holidays R
Huxley Coaches R, M, H, BF
Incentive Travel R, M, BF
Jay Tours Travel R, H
Kirby's Coaches R, M, BF
Leger Travel R, M, H
Lothian Region Transport plc R, M
Moswin Tours R, M, BF, RR etc.
National Holidays/Smiths Shearings R, M, BF, H, Bav
Nettleton Travel Services R
Newell's Travel R, M, H
Page & Moy Limited R, M, H, BF
Parrys Coastline Holidays R, M, BF
Plaid Travel R, M, BF
Redfern Travel Group R
Redwoods Travel R, Bav
Renown Coach Tours Bav
Roman City Holidays R, RR
Rover European Travel R
Rules Coaches Limited R, M, H
Saga Holidays (over 60s) R, Bav
St. Martin's Travel Limited R, M
Selwyns Travel Limited R
Shelton Orsborn R, M, Bav
Skills Motor Coaches Limited R
Southern Tourist Services R
Stirling, Sunrise, Streamline & Anglia R, M
Suntan Holidays R, M
Suntrader Travel R, M, H
Sussex Leamland Limited R, Bav
Swansdown Coaches R
Tappins Holidays R, M
Titan Travel Limited R, M, Bav
Travelahead Limited R, M, BF
Travelscene Limited R, M
Travelsphere Limited R, M, BF, Con

Ulsterbus Tours R, M
Vision Travel Limited R, M, Bav
Voel Coaches R, M
Wallace Arnold R, M, BF, H, Bav
Walsh Travel Limited R, M, BF
Warner Fairfax R, M
E.T. White & Sons Limited M, BF, Ham
Woods Coaches Limited R
Worthing Coaches R, M, BF, Bav
Wrays of Harrogate R, M, H
Wyresdale Coaches R, BF, H
Yateley Travel R, BF
York Tours & Holidays BF

Cruises

Some of the *Rhine and Mosel Valley* tours also include an element of cruising. Most of these involve a coach tour to a starting point on the river, a cruise and a coach ride back home. Many of them use the *KD German Rhine Line* boats. This company also offer their own cruise holidays including a "Connoisseurs Cruise" on which you travel by air to *Cologne*, cruise up and down the river and return to *Cologne* for your flight home. There is also a "Jewels of Europe" cruise which starts with rail travel on the Orient Express and includes a cruise from *Zürich* down river to *Düsseldorf*. The "Cruise to Switzerland" starts from *Cologne* and can include a stay in Switzerland if you wish. A holiday called "Vive La France" is an air/cruise from *Düsseldorf* to *Strasbourg* and on to *Paris*.

Companies in this country which will arrange cruises, air/cruises or coach/cruises on the Rhine and Mosel include:

> **Airsprung Travel Ltd**
> **Antler Holidays**
> **Applebys Coaches**
> **Baxter Travel**
> **British Rhine & Moselle Cruises**
> **Canterbury Travel**

The Caravan Club
Cosmos Tours Limited
Cotsworld Travel Limited
Cruising Incorporated
DER Travel Service
European Yacht Cruises Limited
Feenstrsa Rhine Line
Festive Holidays Limited
KD German Rhine Line
Moswin Tours
National Holidays
Page and Moy Limited
Renaissance Tours Limited
St Martin's Travel Limited
Scandinavian Seaways
Stirling, Sunrise, Streamline & Anglia
Swan Hellenic
Taber Holidays
Travelscene Limited
Travelsphere Limited
Vision Travel Limited
Voel Coaches
Wallace Arnold/Global

Fred Olson Holidays, Swan Hellenic, and **GTF Tours** also offer air/cruises which start with a flight to *Munich* and include cruising on the *Danube* to *Budapest* and *Vienna*.

Serenissima Travel Limited have a special *Danube* air/ cruise which includes three tickets for operas and concerts.

Canterbury Travel also have an air/rail/cruise on the *Elbe* and *Weser* which sounds unusual and interesting. **Swan Hellenic** have a cruise to the Baltic capitals which includes visits to *Hamburg, Kiel* and *Lübeck*.

Rail holidays
Some of the Rhine Cruises can begin with rail travel to your

boarding point. **Canterbury Travel**, in particular, offer this alternative.

DER Travel Service have holidays by air or rail to many parts of the country, including the *Black Forest, Neckar, Franconia, Rhine, Mosel, Bavaria, Northern Germany* and *Lake Constance*, or they will obtain a DB Tourist Rail Rover Card for you so that you can explore the entire country.

Other companies which arrange holidays with rail travel include:

Angel Travel
Golden Arrow Travel
Moswin Tours
Nord-West Travel
Taber Holidays

CHAPTER TWENTY:
SPECIAL INTEREST HOLIDAYS

More and more people these days are tiring of weeks spent lying on the beach and are looking for holidays which offer activities and experiences which will give interest and enjoyment. The travel companies which advertise holidays in Germany cover a wide range of interests and offer many different ways of filling that precious holiday time.

Language courses

If you would like to combine a holiday with a chance to learn, or improve your command of, the German language, **Moswin Tours** have a coach trip called a German Language/Romantic Road tour which is based at *Wemding* near *Nördlingen*.

Euro Academy Limited have courses for many different levels of competency based in several German towns and will arrange travel by rail or air.

If you prefer to make your own travel arrangements the **Goethe Institut** have intensive language courses for adults in centres all over Germany including special courses for commercial correspondence, economics and medicine.

Cultural and Educational Services Abroad have language courses for juniors and adults, students and business people in various towns and cities.

Wine and beer tours

The appreciation and enjoyment which so many people get from drinking German wines has led several companies to offer holidays which combine visits to famous vineyards with wine tastings and seminars on wine production. Two companies listed in the GNTO brochure are **World Wine Tours Limited** and **Vintage Wine Tours**. Both have pre-planned packages or they will tailor-make an itinerary to suit individual requirements. For more basic wine tasting tours, you could join one of the many coach trips or cruises which incorporate wine tasting and wine festival visits. These include:

> **Canterbury Travel**
> **H.E Craiggs-Wansbeck Coaches**
> **Galloway Travel Limited**
> **IMP Travel**
> **Moswin Tours**
> **Page and Moy**
> **Redfern Travel Group**
> **Rover European Travel**
> **Vision Travel Limited**
> **Wallace Arnold/Global**
> **Walsh Travel Limited**
> **Warner Fairfax**
> **E.B. White & Sons Limited**
> **Wrays of Harrogate**
> **Yateley Travel**

For beer drinkers, **CAMRA** offer a Beer Tour to *Düsseldorf, Bamberg* and *Munich*, timed to coincide with the *Oktoberfest*.

Southern Tourist Services have a September visit to the Beer Festival in *Ulm*.

Other educational holiday courses

A.C.E. Study Tours have a coach trip called "German Romanesque".

Anglophile offer "Romans and Romanesque in the Rhineland" and a trip to southern Germany and the *Danube* to study the archaeology and culture of the region.

DER have a History Lover's air or rail holiday to *Regensburg* and *Passau*.

Moswin Tours have a geological tour of southern Germany by coach, a "Roman Art and Treasures of the Mosel" trip and a special *Black Forest* holiday which includes skiing and art classes if you wish.

Plantaganet Tours have a trip devoted to the medieval German emperors on which holiday makers are accompanied by a professor.

Martin Randall Travel have an air and coach tour of Baroque and Rococo Germany in the *Munich* area with excursions to several places of interest.

Christmas visits

Several companies arrange trips to the famous German Christmas markets.

Rover European Travel Limited have a coach trip to the *Nuremberg Christkindlmarkt* which includes an excursion to *Rothenburg*.

Moswin Tours offer several Christmas trips including the *Bernkastel* medieval Christmas market, a "Christmas in the Black Forest" holiday staying in *Schluchsee*, and a "Romantic Road Christmas" which includes *Nuremberg*.'

Countrywide Holidays go to *Rothenburg and the Romantic Road* for Christmas both by coach and by air.

Galaxy Holidays list a coach trip called "Snowtime in Bavaria".

DER have air or rail travel to the Christmas markets in *Nuremberg* or *Frankfurt* and Christmas holidays in *Bavaria, the Black Forest* or *Rhine Valley*.

DA Tours suggest spending the New Year in *Heidelberg*.

Crusader Holidays have a Rhineland Christmas holiday to *Boppard* by coach.

Applegates Supreme Coaches choose the Christmas market at *Brodenbach* on the *Mosel*.

Martin Randall Travel go to *Franconia* for Christmas and include excursions to places of historical and architectural interest.

167

Tour de Force have a Christmas visit to *Heidelberg*.

Holidays for the disabled

Carefree Holidays arrange special trips for the disabled in the *Rhine* and *Mosel* valleys.

MPH Travel have holidays in *Cologne* and the *Rhine/ Mosel* valleys for the mentally or physically handicapped and their friends.

Walking holidays

Some travel firms will arrange walking tours by rail or with your own car.

Russell Hafter Holidays have a tour between the *Main* and *Danube* including *Detwang, Dinkelsbühl* and *Schillingfürst* or "In the steps of King Ludwig" which includes most of his famous castles.

Waymark Holidays arrange trips for walkers and take them to their starting points by air or coach.

A slightly different tour is arranged by **DER**. Called a "Nature Lover's Holiday" it is an air and car tour centred around *Prien* and *Chiemsee* in Bavaria.

Battlefield tours

There is even a company run by **Major and Mrs Holt** who will arrange for you to tour the battlefields of the *Rhine* crossing, the *Munich/Nuremberg/Berchtesgaden* area or "Both sides of the Berlin Wall' complete with guest lecturers.

Tours for railway/transport enthusiasts

TEFS Travel Service have arranged special interest "to Europe for Steam" tours to *Nuremberg, Frankfurt* and *Munich* by air to enable enthusiasts to enjoy the steam trains still used in the area. And **World Steam Ltd** have a variety of holidays for steam enthusiasts.

Nettleton Travel Services have a coach trip to *Nuremberg* which includes a visit to the *Neuenmarkt Wirsberg* steam train museum and the German transport museum. They also go to *Assmannshausen* to visit the preserved steam railway and the *Lahn* valley funicular.

Cycle and motor cycle tours

Eurobike arrange continental touring holidays which include ferry crossing and accomodation in guest houses, hotels, farmhouses or campsites for people with their own motorcycles.

European Adventure Motorcycle Tours have a programme of tours in different parts of the country. Once again you need your own bike.

Bents Bicycle Tours arrange holidays using plane or bus travel which include the transfer of your luggage between hotels, the use of a bicycle and visits to places of interest along the route.

APPENDIX ONE :
ADDRESSES OF REGIONAL TOURIST
OFFICES

SCHLESWIG-HOLSTEIN
- Fremdenverkehrsverband Schleswig-Holstein e V.
  Niemannsweg 31, D-2300 KIEL 1

HAMBURG
- Fremdenverkehrszentrale Hamburg e V.
  Bieberhaus/am Bahnhof, D-2000 HAMBURG 1

LOWER SAXONY
- Landesfremdenverkehrsverband Niedersachen
  Markstrasse 45 (Gildehaus) D-3380   GOSLAR 1

NORTH SEA-LOWER SAXONY-BREMEN
- Fremdenverkehrsverband Nordsee-Niedersachen-
  Bremen e V.
  Gottorpstrasse 18, Postfach 1820,
  D-2900 OLDENBURG

LUNEBERG HEATH
- Fremdenverkehrsverband Lüneberger Heide e V.
  Glockenhaus, Postfach 2160, D-2120 LUNEBERG

WESER HILLS
- Fremdenverkehrsverband Weserbergland-
  Mittelweser e V.
  Falkestrasse 2, Postfach 174, D-3250 HAMELN

WESTPHALIA
- Landesverkehrsverband Westfalen e V.
  Südwall 6, D-4600 DORTMUND

RHINELAND
- Landesverkehrsverband Rheinland e V.
  Rheinallee 69, Postfach 20 08 61, D-5300 BONN 2

RHINELAND-PALATINATE
- Fremdenverkehrsverband Rheinland Pfalz e V.
  Löhrstr 103-105, Postfach 1420, D-5400 KOBLENZ

SAAR
- Fremdenverkehrsverband Saarland e V.
  Am Stiefel 2, Postfach 242, D-6600 SAARBRÜCKEN 3

HESSE
- Hessische Landeszentrale für Fremdenverkehr
  Abraham-Lincoln-Strasse 38-42, D-6200 WIESBADEN

BADEN-WÜRTTEMBERG
- Landesfremdenverkehrsverband Baden-
  Württemberg e V.
  Bussenstrasse 23, D-7000 STUTTGART
- Fremdenverkehrsverband Schwarzwald e V.
  Bertoldstrasse 45, Postfach 16 60, D-7800 FREIBURG
- Fremdenverkehrsverband Neckarland-Schwaben e V.
  Am Wollhaus 14, D-7100 HEILBRONN
- Fremdenverkehrsverband Bodensee-Oberschwaben e V.
  Schützenstrasse 8, D-7750 KONSTANZ

BAVARIA
- Landesfremdenverkehrsverband Bayern e V.
  Prinzregentenstrasse 18, Postfach 22 04 40,
  D-8000 MÜNCHEN 22
- Fremdenverkehrsverband Franken e V.
  Postfach 269, D-8500 NÜRNBERG 18
- Fremdenverkehrsverband Ostbayern e V.
  Landshuterstrasse 13, D-8400 REGENSBURG
- Fremdenverkehrsverband München Oberbayern e V.
  Sonnenstrasse 10, Postfach 20 09 29,
  D-8000 MÜNCHEN 2
- Fremdenverkehrsverband Allgäu/Bayerisch-
  Schwaben e V
  Fuggerstrasse 9, D-8900 AUGSBURG 1

APPENDIX TWO:
ADDRESSES OF HOTEL CHAINS WITH BRANCHES OR ASSOCIATES IN GERMANY

Best Western/Unitels
Vine House, 143 London Road
Kingston-upon-Thames KT2 6NA
Tel: 01-541 0033

Concorde Hotels
5 Victoria Road
London W8
Tel: 01-937 8033

CP Canadian Pacific Hotels
62-65 Trafalgar Square
London WC2N 5DY
Tel: 01-798 9898

Crest Hotels
Bridge Street
Banbury
OX16 8RQ
Tel: 0295-25255

Dorint Hotels
16 Bedford Square
London WC1B 3JA
Tel: 01-323 0898

Golden Tulip International
655 London Road
Isleworth, Middx TW7 4ET
Tel: 01-847 3951

Hilton International
6 Bedford Avenue
London WC1B 3HY
Tel: 01-631 1767

Holiday Inns Reservations
10-12 New College Parade
Finchley Road, London NW3 5EP

Intercontinental Hotels/Forum Hotels International
Thameside Centre, Kew Bridge Road
Brentford, Middx TW8 OEB
Tel: 01-741 9000

The Leading Hotels of the World/Kempinski Hotels
15 New Bridge Street
London EC4V 6AU
Tel: 0800-181123

Marriott Hotels and Resorts
44 Earlham Street
London WC2H 9LA
Tel: 01-379 7945

Minotels
325 Dickson Road
Blackpool FY1 2JL
Tel: 0253-594185

Penta Hotels
Heathrow Penta Hotel
International Reservations
Room G021, Bath Road,
Hounslow, Middx TW6 2AQ
Tel: 01-897 0551

Pullman International Hotels
c/o Great Eastern Hotel
Suite 96, Liverpool Street
London EC2M 7QN
Tel: 01-621 1962

Queens Moat Houses
Queens Court, 9-17 Eastern Road
Romford, Essex RM1 3NG
Tel: 0800-289330

Ramada International Hotels
160 Brompton Road
London SW3 1HS
Tel: 01-235 5264

ResinTer International Reservations Office
(for Novotel and Ibis Hotels)
1 Shortlands Road, London W6 9DR
Tel: 01-724 1000

Sheraton Reservations Corporation
Kiln House, 210 New Kings Road
London SW6 4NZ
Tel: 0800-353535

Trusthouse Forte
23 – 30 New Street
Aylesbury, Bucks HP20 2NW
Tel: 01-567 3444

APPENDIX THREE:
HOLIDAY COMPANIES AND TOUR OPERATORS

You will not find brochures from most of these companies on the shelves in your local travel agency so it will be necessary to contact them directly if you are interested in the sort of holidays they offer. This list has been drawn up with the generous help of the German National Tourist Office. For current information, particularly in view of the current state of the holiday market, it would be wise to ask them for their most up-to-date list.

A.C.E. Study Tours, Babraham, Cambridge CB2 4AP

Air Foyle Executive Limited, Escapade Division, Halcyon House, Luton Airport, Luton LU2 9LU

Airsprung Travel Ltd, 7 Church Walk, Trowbridge, Wilts BA14 8DX

Albany Travel (Manchester) Ltd, 190 Deansgate, Manchester M3 3WD

Angel Travel Ltd, 34 High Street, Borough Green, Sevenoaks, Kent TN15 8BJ

Angela Holidays, Oaktree Cottages, Lowford, Bursledon, Southampton SO3 8ES

Anglophile, Grange Cottage, Gaters Land, Winterbourne Dauntsey, Salisbury SP4 6EW

Antler Holidays Limited, 5 Upper Brook Street, Rugeley, Staffs WS15 2DP

Applebys Coaches, Conisholme, Louth, Lincs LN11 7LT

Applegates Supreme Coaches, Heathfield Garage, Newport, Berkeley, Glos

Arena Travel, Hamilton House, Cambridge Road,
  Felixstowe, Suffolk IP11 7EU
Arvonia Coaches, The Square, Llanrug, Caernarfon,
  Gwynedd
Auto Plan Holidays Limited, Energy House, Lombard
  Street, Lichfield, Staffs WS13 6DP
Autotours (UK) Limited, 20 Craven Terrace, London
W2 3QH

B and H Travel Services Ltd, 276 Church Road, Sheldon,
  Birmingham B26 3YH
Bakers Dolphine Tours, 21 Penn Street, Broadmead,
  Bristol, Avon BS1 3AU
Baxter Travel, 23 Market Place, Holt, Norfolk NR25 6BE
Bebb Travel, The Coach Station, Llantwit Fardre,
  Pontypridd, Mid Glam CF38 2HB
Bents Bicycle Tours, 65 Grove Road, Harpenden, Herts
  AL5 1EN
Bluebird Coaches, Bus Station, Callendar Riggs, Falkirk,
  Scotland
Breakaways, 149 Ipsley Street, Redditch B98 7AA
British Rhine & Moselle Cruises, 49 South Canterbury
  Road, Canterbury, Kent CT1 3LH
Buckby's Coaches, 1 Bridge Street, Rothwell, Kettering,
  Northants
Business and Trade Fair Travel Limited, 2 Majestic Parade,
  Sandgate Road, Folkestone, Kent

Camra Travel Club c/o Arblaster & Clarke, 104 Church
  Road, Steep, Petersfield, Hants GU32 2DD
Canterbury Travel, 248 Streatfield Road, Harrow HA3 9BY
Canvas Holidays Limited, Bull Plain, Hertford, Herts
  SG14 1DY
The Caravan Club, East Grinstead House, East Grinstead,
  West Sussex RH19 1UA
Carefree Holidays Limited, 64 Florence Road,
  Northampton NN1 4NA

Cavendish Travel, c/o Dowtours, 230 High Street, Herne Bay, Kent CT6 5AX

Central Liner, West Midlands Travel Ltd, Miller Street, Aston, Birmingham B6 4NG

Charnwood Travel Limited, 32 Horley Row, Horley, Surrey RH6 8DH

Chequers Travel Ltd, Newbridge House, Newbridge, Dover, Kent CT16 1YS

City Cruiser Holidays Limited, 29/31 Leicester Street, Bedworth, Warwicks CV12 8JP

Club Relax International, 521 Watford Road, St. Albans, Herts AL2 3DU

Club Cantabrica Coaches Limited, 9 Elton Way, Watford, Herts WD2 8HH

Contiki Travel (UK) Limited, Wells House, 15 Elmfield Road, Bromley, Kent BR1 1LS

Cosmos Tours Ltd, Tourama House, 17 Homesdale Road, Bromley, Kent BR2 9LX

Cotsworld Travel Limited, Eastgate Chambers, Market Way, Eastgate Street, Gloucester GL1 1QQ

Countrywide Holidays, Birch Heys, Cromwell Range, Manchester M14 6HU

H.E. Craiggs-Wansbeck Coaches, Main Road, Radcliffe, Northumberland NE65 0JB

Cresta Holidays, Cresta House, 32 Victoria Street, Altrincham, Cheshire

Cruising Incorporated, 1 Portland Road, Bath BA1 2SJ

Crusader Holidays, 78/80 Pier Avenue, Clacton-on-Sea, Essex CO15 1NH

Cultural and Educational Services Abroad, 44 Sydney Street, Brighton, Sussex BN1 4EP

DA Tours, Williamton House, Low Causeway, Culross, Fife KY12 8HL

Dalesman Holidays, 9 Leeds Road, Ilkley, West Yorks LS29 8DH

David Newman's European Collection, Box 733, 40 Upperton Road, Eastbourne, Sussex BN21 4AW

Davidson Travel, 103 Carston Close, Lee, London
   SW12 8DX
Davies Bros. International Tours, Blossom Garage,
   Pencader, Dyfed SA39 9HA
Dawson & Sanderson, 26 Ridley Place, Newcastle-upon-
   Tyne NE1 8JW
DER Travel Service, 18 Conduit Street, London W1R 9DT
Dopple M European, Suite A, Troy House, Elmgrove
   Road, Harrow, Middx HA1 2QQ

Elsey's Tours Limited, The Travel Centre, High Street,
   Gosberton, near Spalding, Lincs PE11 4NA
Emblings Coaches, Bridge Garage, Guyhirn, Wisbech,
   Cambs
Epsom Coaches, Blenheim Road, Longmead Estate, Epsom,
   Surrey KT19 9AF
Euro Academy Ltd, 77a George Street, Croydon CR0 1LD
Eurobike, The Riverside Centre, 46 High Street, Kingston-
   upon-Thames, Surrey KT1 1HN
Eurocamp Travel Ltd, Edmundson House, Tatton Street,
   Knutsford, Cheshire WA16 6BG
European Adventure Motorcycle Tours, 8a Sandy Lane,
   Prestatyn, Clwyd LL19 7SG
European Yacht Cruises Ltd, 28 Station Approach,
   Hayes, Bromley, Kent BR2 7EH
Eurotours, Hall Autos, 64 Station Road, Wallsend,
   Newcastle-upon-Tyne NE28 6TB
Excelsior Holidays, Excelsior House, 22a Sea Road,
   Bournemouth BH5 1DD
EXPO Travel Services Limited, 35 Piccadilly, London
   W1V 9PB

Feenstra Rhine Line c/o Dovehouse Travel, 377 Warwick
   Road, Olton, Solihull, West Midlands B91 1BQ
Festive Holidays Ltd, Acorn House, Great Oaks,
   Basildon, Essex SS14 1AH
Fitzcharles Coaches Limited, Newkerse Garage,
87 Newhouse Road, Grangemouth FK3 8NJ

Fred Olson Holidays, Crown House, Crown Street,
Ipswich, Suffolk IP1 3HB

Gain Travel Experience Limited, 6 Fair Road, Wibsey,
Bradford BD6 1QN

Galaxy Holidays, Pillar & Lucy House, Merchants Road,
Gloucester GL1 5RG

Galloway Travel Ltd, Mendlesham, Stowmarket, Suffolk

German Tourist Facilities, 182-186 Kensington Church
Street, London W8 4DP

German Travel Agency, 18 West Bute Street, Cardiff
CF1 6EP

Globepost Travel Services, 324 Kennington Park Road,
London SE11 4PD

Goethe Institut, 50 Princes Gate, Exhibition Road,
London SW7 2PH

Golden Arrow Travel, 76 High Street, Tunbridge Wells,
Kent TN1 1YB

Tony Goss Travel, 3 Somerset Place, Totnes, Devon
TQ9 5AX

Go Whittle, 105 Coventry Street, Kidderminster, Worcs
DY10 2BH

Grand UK Holidays, 6 Exchange Street, Norwich
NR2 1AT

Russell Hafter Holidays, 26 The Square, Ashfield,
Dunblane FK15 OJN

Halcyon Travel, Halcyon House, Wincolmlee, Hull
HU2 8HT

Hamilton Travel, 3 Heddon Street, London W1R 7LE

Happy Days Coaches, Woodseaves, Stafford ST20 OJR

Harris Coaches, Manor Road, West Thurrock, Grays,
Essex RM16 1EH

Harrison Holidays, Orchard Lane, Gaywood, King's
Lynn, Norfolk

Heartland Holidays Limited, 18 Shakespeare Road,
Harpenden, Herts AL5 5NQ

G.W. Henebery Ltd, Personal Opera Tours, Kareol, Islip,
  Oxford OX5 2SU
Heritage Travel, 21 Dorset Square, London NW1 6QG
Holiday Coach, 16-21 North Lane, Canterbury, Kent
CT2 7DX
Major and Mrs Holt's Battlefield Tours, Golden Key
  Building, 15 Market Street, Sandwich, Kent CT13 9DA
Hoseasons Holidays Abroad Limited, Sunway House,
  Lowestoft, Suffolk NR32 3LT
Hoverland European Holidays, 61 Bradford Street,
  Walsall, West Midlands WS1 3QD
Hoverspeed Limited, Maybrook House, Queens Gardens,
  Dover, Kent CT17 9UQ
Huxley Coaches, Rose Cottage, Threapwood, Malpas,
  Cheshire SY14 7AT

Ian Allen Travel Limited, Terminal House, Shepperton,
  Middx
IEL Travel, 9 Argyll Street, London W1V 2HA
IMP Travel, 17 Sincil Street, Lincoln LN5 7ET
Incentive Travel, 85 London Road, Marks Tey, Essex
  CO6 1EB
Intasun, Citybreaks, PO Box 228, Bromley, Kent
  BR1 1LA
Interhome Limited, 383 Richmond Road, Twickenham
  TW1 2EF

Jay Tours Travel, 30 King Street, Alfreton, Derbys
  DE55 7AG

KD German Rhine Line, 28 South Street, Epsom, Surrey
  KT18 7PF
Kirby's Coaches, Princess Road, Rayleigh, Essex
  SS6 8HR

Leger Travel, 75 Kirkgate, Wakefield WF1 1HX
LEP Fairs, Unit 18, 3rd Exhibition Avenue, National
  Exhibition Centre, Birmingham B40 1PJ

LIMO (LEP International Meeting Organisers Limited), International House, 20 Dudley Road, Tunbridge Wells, Kent TN1 1LF

Lothian Regional Transport plc, 14 Queen Street, Edinburgh EH2 1JL

Magnum Holidays, 7 Westleigh Park, Blaby, Leicester LE8 3EL

Martin Randall Travel, 10 Barley Mow Passage, Chiswick, London W4 4PH

MGP (Special Event Travel), White Lion House, Shortgate, Lewes, East Sussex BN8 6PJ

Moswin Tours, PO Box 8, 52b London Road, Oadby, Leicester LE2 5WX

MPH Travel Club, 12 Saxon Street, Dover, Kent CT17 9RT

National Express, 4 Vicarage Road, Edgbaston, Birmingham B15 3ES

National Holidays/Smiths Shearings, Miry Lane, Wigan, Lancs WN3 4AG

Nettleton Travel Services, 10 Manor Street, Otley, West Yorks LS21 1AX

Newell's Travel, 29a Fore Street, Redruth, Cornwall TR15 2BQ

Nord-West Travel, 43 Bayley Road, Willaton, Nantwich, Cheshire CW5 6RL

North Sea Ferries, King George Dock, Hedon Road, Hull HU9 5QA

Olau Line (UK) Limited, Sheerness, Kent ME12 1SN

Onspec Tours, 6 Eversfield Road, Eastbourne, East Sussex BN21 2AS

Overdrive Holidays, 50 Morthern Road, Wickersley, South Yorks S66 OEN

Page and Moy Ltd, 136/140 London Road, Leicester LE2 1EN

Parrys Coastline Holidays, 29 Station Street, Cheslyn
  Hay, Walsall, W. Midlands WS6 7ED
Party and Business Travel Limited, 37 Klondyke Trading
  Estate, Rushenden Road, Queenborough ME11 5HH
Pegasus Holidays Ltd, River House, Restmor Way,
  Hackbridge Road, Wallington, Surrey SM6 7AH
Plaid Travel, Buccleuch Road, Selkirk TD7 5DL Scotland
Plantagenet Tours, c/o Peter Gravegaard, 85 The Grove,
  Moordown, Bournemouth, Dorset BH9 2TY
P & O European Ferries, Channel House, Channel View
  Road, Dover, Kent CT17 9TJ
Prospect Music and Arts Ltd, 10 Barley Mow Passage,
  London W4 4PH

RAC Motoring Services, RAC House, PO Box 100,
  Bartlett Street, South Croydon CR2 6XW
Redfern Travel Group, Lindley Street, Mansfield, Notts
  NG18 1QE
Redwoods Travel, Fairview, Hemyock, Cullompton,
  Devon EX15 3QR
Renaissance Tours Ltd, Middleburg Square, Folkestone,
  Kent CT20 1AZ
Renown Coach Tours, 22 Station Road, Bexhill-on-Sea,
  Sussex
Roman City Holidays, 53 High Street, Thornbury, Bristol
  BS12 2AW
Rover European Travel Limited, The Coach House,
  Horsely, Stroud, Glos GL6 0PU
Rules Coaches Ltd, Riverside, Boxford, Colchester, Essex

SAGA Holidays, The Saga Building, Middelburg Square,
  Folkestone, Kent CT20 1AZ
St. Martin's Travel Ltd, 37 St. Martin's Court, London
  WC2N 4AL
Sally Holidays, Argyle Centre, York Street, Ramsgate,
  Kent CT11 9DS
Scandinavian Seaways, Parkeston Quay, Harwich, Essex
  CO12 4QG

Sealink Holidays, Charter House, Park Street, Ashford, Kent TN24 8EX

Select Site Reservations, Travel House, Pandy, nr Abergavenny, Gwent NP7 8DH

Selwyn's Travel Limited, Cormorant Drive, Picow Farm Road Industrial Estate, Runcorn, Cheshire WA7 4UD

Serenissima Travel Ltd, 21 Dorset Square, London NW1 6QG

Shelton Orsborn, London Road, Wollaston, Northants NN9 7QR

Skills Motor Coaches Limited, 1 St Peter's Street, Nottingham NG7 3EL

Southern Tourist Services, 4 Grosvenor Close, Ashley Heath, Ringwood, Hants BH24 2HG

Sports Spectator International Limited, 1 Sycamore Road, Amersham, Bucks HP6 5EQ

Sportsmans Travel Limited, PO Box 269, Brentwood, Essex CM15 8NR

Stirling, Sunrise, Streamline & Anglia, St. Mary's House, Duke Street, Norwich NR3 1PT

Suntan Holidays, 104 Regent Road, Great Yarmouth, Norfolk NR30 2AH

Suntrader Travel, 253 Holdenhurst Road, Bournemouth BH8 8DA

Sussex Leamland Ltd., 2 Arcade Buildings, South Street, Worthing BN11 3AY

Swan Hellenic, 77 New Oxford Street, London WC1A 1PP

Swansdown Coaches, The House of Travel, 1 The Broadway, Thatcham, Newbury

Taber Holidays, Norway House, 126 Sunbridge Road, Bradford, West Yorkshire BD1 2SX

Tappins Holidays, Station Road, Didcot, Oxon OX11 7LZ

TEFS Travel Service, "to Europe for Steam", Loughborough, Leics LE11 3TL

Titan Travel Limited, Hartland House, 43 Church Street, Reigate, Surrey RH2 OAH

Tourauto Holidays, Bridge House, Ware, Herts SG12 9DF

Tour de Force, 71 Oxford Street, London W1R 1RB

Travelahead Ltd, 22 Huntingdon Close, Totton,
Southampton SO4 3NX

The Travel Force, High Street, Leicester LE1 5YW

Travelscene Ltd., Travelscene House, 11/15 St. Ann's
Road, Harrow, Middx. HA1 1AS

Tracks Europe, The Flots, Brookland, Romney Marsh,
Kent TN29 9TG

Travelsphere Ltd, Compass House, Coventry Road, Market
Harborough, Leics LE16 9BZ

Ulsterbus Tours, 10 Glengall Street, Belfast BT12 5AH

Unicorn Holidays, Intech House, 34-35 Cam Centre,
Wilbury Way, Hitchin, Herts SG4 0RL

Vintage Wine Tours, 8 Belmont, Lansdown Road, Bath
BA1 5DZ

VIP Travel Limited, 42 North Audley Street, Grosvenor
Square, London W1A 4PY

Vision Travel Ltd, 118a Hamilton Road, Felixstowe,
Suffolk IP11 7AB

Voel Coaches, Dyserth, Rhyl, Clwyd LL18 6BP

Wallace Arnold/Global, Gelderd Road, Leeds LS12 6DH

Walsh Travel Ltd, 8 Kyle Street, Ayr KA7 IRZ Scotland

Warner Fairfax, Oldbury Buildings, Northway Lane,
Tewkesbury, Glos GL20 8JG

Waymark Holidays, 295 Lillie Road, London SW6 7LL

E.T. White & Sons Ltd, Flint House Garage, Calver, nr.
Sheffield S30 1XH

Woods Coaches Limited, Bedford Road, Wigston, Leicester
LE8 2XD

World Steam Ltd, 3 Shadwell Grove, Radcliffe on Trent,
Nottingham NG12 2ET

World Wine Tours Limited, 4 Dorchester Road, Drayton,
St. Leonard, Oxon OX9 8BH

Worthing Coaches, 117 George V Avenue, Worthing, W.
Sussex BN11 5SA

Wrays of Harrogate, 33 Montpelier Parade, Harrogate,
  N. Yorks HG1 2TG
Wyresdale Coaches, Green Lane, Garstang, nr. Preston
  PR3 1NJ

Yateley Travel, Yateley, Camberley, Surrey GU17 7UW
York Tours & Holidays, Town Centre House, 8 Mercer's
  Row, Northampton NN1 2QL

Index of Place names